RISE OF THE
NEW WORLD ORDER 3

THE GREAT RESET

J. MICHAEL THOMAS HAYS

TABLE OF CONTENTS

PREFACE

Hello, friend.

I'm sorry to say we're not meeting under the best of circumstances, but I probably didn't need to tell you that after all we've been through since I released **Rise of the New World Order 2: The Awakening** back in 2015.

I'm afraid the sinister agenda for the culling of man has been set in motion.

I was hoping for my kids' sake that this wouldn't have come so soon, but it has, and this is why ten years ago I named my first book, "Rise of the New World Order 1: The Culling of Man".

If you read my first book pre-pandemic you surely refused the euthanizing injections, of which long-term side effects of sudden death are showing up in waves right now as you read this.

Unfortunately for all of us, it's all part of the Great Plan.

As always with my books, listen to what I have to say and then do your due diligence researching for yourself what I've said. I'm just telling you what I believe and why. Make sure you come to your own conclusions.

I am still displaying Old Glory upside down on the back of this third book because we are under attack more than ever by the proponents of the Great Plan, the Illuminati.

If you have not read at least my first book I implore you to do so that you may understand this book and the reasons for the events that have happened over the last few years and more that are at our doorstep.

I'm going to assume you have read my first book and are on board with what I've already said and gone over. In other words, I'm not going to repeat "if you'll remember from my first book" over and over ad nauseum. We're past all that. You already know what I'm talking about and we'll save the space.

I'm still author-editor and I literally don't write books for a living...yet.

Apologies in advance if I seem to repeat myself here or there but that just means I'm just hammering a point home, right? Right.

Now, this personal event I'm going to tell you about is related to an incident you'll remember from my first book (!) about a supernatural experience that transfigured me from a lifelong atheist into a Sentinel of Jesus through my knowledge of things to do with the New World Order, and especially the mechanics of the Great Plan.

The degree of disturbing truth about the origination and execution of the Great Plan was what really set me free to re-think everything I had thought I'd know all my life, especially my atheism. It seemed that we were part of a Grand Play that has been going on for about 6,000 years now and I believe we're at the threshold of the raising of the curtain for the Grand Finale....the appearance of the Antichrist and the return of Jesus.

When I was fully awakened to the dark truth about King Nimrod and the Babylonian Mystery Religion (Mystery Babylon from Revelation), the fog I was unable to see through up to that point to finish putting all the conspiracy puzzle pieces together dissipated. Everything that didn't click before suddenly did.

A couple years before all this supernatural-spiritual stuff happened to me, I had 'woken up' to the ugly truth of the factual existence of the "New World Order" conspiracy against mankind: Wealthy globalist-eugenicists were conspiring behind the scenes using secret societies to try and take over the world and were about to succeed.

I initially woke up in 2007 by learning about the backstory behind the unconstitutional, illegal, privately-owned, for-profit Federal

Reserve, and also the peculiar and critically important facts surrounding the events of 9/11 that DIDN'T make it into the mainstream media.

The moment I saw the video that a 47-story skyscraper collapsed in New York the evening of 9/11 that hadn't even been hit by a jet I was floored. That was an impossibility in my mind. How did I not hear about this? "There was nothing on the news about this" I thought to myself.

I didn't believe it at first but when I looked it up it was true and I suddenly felt ill and it was like I just entered a bad, bad dream...but I was wide awake.

The more I learned the suppressed, forbidden truth about who runs our world and how corrupt it is, the more it seemed I was sinking in a pit of despair...how much worse is this news going to get??

After initially learning the truth about Building 7 from 9/11, I felt like someone had kicked me right in the stomach. I didn't sleep a wink that night I was so wigged out. Days passed and it progressed from there. The closest feeling I could relate to what I was going through was like the heartbreak you feel when a love goes sour, or you lose a close, loved one.

I felt s-o-o-o-o betrayed by everything that had come before me up to that moment. The school system. The media. The government. How was this kept from me for so long? And the others. Then I started learning how and why.

Weeks and months ticked by and my anxiety level maxed out trying to figure out what to do about what I had just learned, and was still learning about daily then.

Well, my temper was boiling after a few weeks of being awake, knowing that there were factually evil people out there in the world conspiring to do me, my family, my country and general humanity great harm and even death and I started researching everything about it so I could figure out how to do something about it...sort through all the BS and get the story straight and into some sort of order of events... find out exactly who is doing this to us...maybe put it all into a book to warn my family and friends and hopefully they would spread the word from there about the Great Plan to enslave all of humanity.

So. I had my mission: Write the best book I could possibly write and show the Great Plan from start to finish so people would be able to understand the conspiracy.

However...

Coming from an atheist point of view, I kept running into a brick wall trying to get to the bottom of it because I wouldn't acknowledge the existence of the supernatural....that which is not of our physical 3D world. You know, like a lot of the stuff from the Bible in particular.

I kept running across people saying Satan and his followers were at the root of all of this mess. There's no way the people running the world could be worshipping Satan I was thinking, that's all fairy tale BS. They must be using that as a cover for being extraterrestrial agents or something like that along the lines of what David Icke was talking about, I thought.

I was forced to go off-and-on to Sunday School at a Presbyterian church as a child until I was old enough to say no, about 14 years old. I then considered myself an atheist who followed facts and science, not fairy tales and make-believe.

I knew the game clock was ticking against us so I launched into my research hardcore, 110% effort. Prosecutor Hays on the case. No stone shall go unturned. I was going to build a factual case to convict whoever was behind this NWO conspiracy.

Many late nights were spent digging and digging and making e-files of different subjects as I went to keep everything ordered, straight and logical.

I was a decent student in high school and despite being highly rebellious and cutting classes a ton I made it out easy with a 3.3 GPA and took many English classes so I knew how to write an organized report on a subject.

I looked at it as writing dozens of mini-reports on all the various subjects and then combining them to flow together in a book.

"I can do this" I told myself. I felt I had no choice.

I started taking the alleged facts about all of it and cross-referencing. Double-checking. Fool me once, shame on you…I wasn't going to get fooled again, not on this level. No way. No how. This was sink or swim, do or die, failure is not an option. My kids and my country were on the line and it was all on my shoulders.

But no matter which video I watched, book I read, interview I listened to, there was nothing but dead ends and conmen largely in that New Age realm of 'conspiracy theory' full of UFOs and reptilians and Pleiadeans and spiritual enlightenment and blah blah blah…and I went through ALL of it until I exhausted every avenue of explanation as to why the people who ruled the world were highly evil, occultists, and appeared to be Satanists in particular at that.

Did. Not. Add. Up. Not at all, and I was about out of research to do in that New Age-extraterrestrial realm. I was just spinning my wheels at that point and about to blow a gasket.

Then I came across the story of King Nimrod and the Babylonian Mystery Religion. Learning about that in particular was the key that unlocked the root truth, and not a peep about this in the New Age arena of "truth."

It took a couple of years and tons of research and in March 2009, after everything I had learned, I could finally and only come to the honest, most reasonable, factual conclusion that actual Satan worshippers rule our world. They literally worship Satan from the Bible...in particular. Satan.

And the only reason they did that was because he was real and to gain his supernatural help in ruling the world as his earthly representatives, and all the money and power due Satan's human representatives on Earth.

And if that was my best, most-factual and logical conclusion based on what I'd learned of the matter then that meant that not only was Satan a real entity, but God and Jesus were real too...yikes.

Totaling up and accepting all the factual evidence related to the Great Plan was my personal way of coming to believe in God.

I vividly remember sitting at my desk about 10 or 11 o'clock in the evening, the Spring of 2009, having this conversation with myself about the facts to do with the New World Order, especially everything about King Nimrod and the Babylonian Mystery Religion. I felt like I was losing my mind to be quite honest.

Now, it's well known in my books that I'm a lifelong construction worker, and still am, and I walk and talk like one. All my life. I was sitting there at my desk in my office, talking to myself out loud, cussing up a storm, pounding on my desk with my fist, as everything I'd learned over the last couple years suddenly started to come together in my mind like a jigsaw puzzle being finished and I started to have this euphoric-crazy-realization-feeling dawning on me.

I started getting really emotional, and began to well-up in my eyes. I could feel something was happening to me physically throughout my whole body.

I was compelled to look straight up at the light above my desk and I had tears streaming down my face and was shaking my head with hands and body trembling.

And I said out loud to God: "You mean You're real?"

And I knew He was then.

I completely broke down crying and then I could immediately feel His supernatural presence and the Holy Spirit was suddenly upon me.

I had literally and figuratively seen the Light. And I was crying then as I'm crying now writing this paragraph, reliving that moment again.

Well, it was quite a rush for someone like me who'd lived a hard and fast life and knew what being high on any number of powerful drugs felt like.

What I was feeling right then and there was a better feeling, a higher high, than anything I'd ever experienced in my life.

I described the **_aftermath_** of this event in my first book, but not the transfiguration itself.

I remember standing in the shower the morning after this happened asking myself "what is going on with me?…it feels like I'm on some kind of crazy drug or something". It was the Holy Spirit radiating within me that I was feeling and I didn't realize it at the time.

It took me a few days to figure it out that the Holy Spirit was causing me to feel like I was, higher than anything in my life. I had just a crazy sense of well-being, 24/7. Like nothing in the world could get me down.

During this time I didn't have any desire to indulge in the vices I'd had all my adult life anymore, they all seemed insignificant and unneeded now.

So unfortunately, me being me, a couple of weeks after getting saved I wondered if that feeling of the Holy Spirit would stick around if I wanted to bring one or two of my vices back on board. So, I decided one night to drink a bunch of beer, smoke a bunch of weed, and basically carry on like an idiot who wanted to have his cake and eat it too.

Well, that was the biggest mistake I've ever made in my life. I was basically testing God.

If I can behave myself and pray regularly and fly straight so I can work on these books I get a taste of that old "on High" feeling, and the longer I live righteously the more the feeling increases. But nothing like those two weeks, it was unreal.

One last personal note here to start with, it's regarding my friend and the artist for my first two book covers, David Dees.

My friend David Dees, fearless anti-NWO artist and activist extraordinaire, passed away from melanoma cancer on May 31, 2020 at 62 years young in Oregon.

Dees distrusted the medical establishment and with good reason, but by the time the pain of his cancer was so bad and he went in to the doctor to get it checked out it was way too late, he had terminal cancer. And he went fast.

I can't help but consider that Dees was intentionally taken out... perhaps zapped in the back with a DEW/Directed Energy Weapon of some sort by the evil ones to cause the rapid onset of a deadly cancer...I don't know. He showed me a picture of the melanoma on his back that killed him, it was a giant, black mole about 3 inches in diameter. Was he literally shot in the back by an assassin? With the reach of his artwork on the internet, he was surely one of the Illuminati's biggest enemies.

It came out in Congressional hearings in the 1970s that the CIA was running around with a 'heart attack gun' that shot a tiny ice bullet with deadly poison that would break down long before an autopsy could be performed. Perfect for taking out the enemies of the Great Plan at that time.

That was the 70s…we're talking 50 years later now. Who knows what kind of diabolical arsenal they have cooked up since then.

All I know for certain is Dees got paroled out of this world and there is a HUGE hole not only in my heart but the Truth Community in general. He was just a gentle, kind, caring soul but a fearless, tenacious, and powerful hero in the information war we continue to fight today.

I first met David online in the Truth Community not long after I released my first book in January of 2013, but I had been a big fan and admirer of his since I first woke up in 2007.

His 'Ron Paul' artwork for the 2008 election drew me right to him and I still like to go back and look at all his old work like that. His 9/11 Truth art was phenomenal. Edgy. Biting. Just so much stuff going on in one image from him. I have all his art books and signed of course, I legit considered him a good friend and he confided in me some pretty crazy stuff!

Dees was a super-patriotic guy too. He knew Ron Paul was our only hope at that time and threw everything he had behind him.

He selflessly gave away his art for free on one hand and lived hand-to-mouth on the other. He really did barely get by because he spent so much time fighting the NWO on his own time and dime. I donated money to him several times, telling him to 'get a pizza and a bottle of wine on me,' and he did.

Thanks for all you did, brother David. Mad respect. The others and I will pick it up for you. Love you, man.

I woke up the next morning with a hangover, and the Holy Spirit had abated me. I felt like I was back in the nightmare of having to face the New World Order…alone.

I think about that now and that also about brings me to the verge of tears.

It's been a non-stop battle now for me that I let those demons back into my camp but I just had to find out, stupid me.

I will believe in God and Jesus and will fight for Them to my end, and surely some elements of the Holy Spirit did stick around despite my haphazardness. I was definitely a changed man after those couple weeks of flying high with God.

CHAPTER 1

NWO COMIN' IN *HOT*

With everything that has happened since 2016 in my own life I barely have had the time to dedicate to research and write another full book, which is why this book 3 took so long to come.

At the end of 2016 I took my own advice and began the great trouble of uprooting and moving my family from a Seattle suburb to about 100 miles further inland and on the other side of the Cascade mountains, a natural buffer. I felt an urgent need to get away from the Seattle-area population center in anticipation of what I believe to be coming.

That meant all new schools for my kids and an unknown work situation for me, we took quite the leap of faith but I felt it had to be done.

I moved us away from the socialist safe-spaces of the hapless citizens of the greater Seattle area into central Washington state, which is largely 'Red State' country. This is where people are much more caring, concerned, friendly, self-sufficient, patriotic and God-fearing than the degenerate horde that took over Seattle since I grew up there in the 70s and 80s.

What a nightmare that place is now. I'd heard that mayors of other major cities have been buying their habitually-reoffending criminals and troubled, drug-addled homeless one-way bus tickets to Seattle, or 'Freeattle' as it's known among the local homeless population.

You walk around Seattle now downtown and it's like walking around the set of "Escape from New York" crossed with "Road Warrior" and I'm not kidding!! Not quite as dangerous, but if and when the power grid goes down those same people will rule the cities and prey upon the unarmed.

So. I went from a house in a Seattle suburb on a postage-stamp-sized lot to a fixer house with a little bit of property…my closest neighbor is 500 feet away..

I now have a big garden. Chickens, geese and ducks, pygmy goats, cats and a horde of misfit dogs no one else would have. Deer by the dozens cross my property daily. I have a private well with the healthiest, best-tasting water ever, with no chlorine or fluoride and only natural minerals.

Neighbors largely keep to themselves but we all rallied together in a heartbeat out of necessity when a truck hit our group mailbox out on the main road and completely destroyed it. We had it back up and running with stronger construction than before within 48 hours.

These are just the kind of people that live in central Washington. Farm country. Cattle country. Blue collar and tough country folk. Hard working people and all armed to the teeth with most of them hunters with the skills and armaments to go along with that. Basically, sharpshooters abound.

This Book 3 you're holding is arguably the final warning to all to batten down the hatches on all fronts. We're on the cusp of events I tried to slow down or even derail by warning people with my books.

I was unsuccessful on that front. People just won't wake up en masse. They are just too distracted, dumbed-down, tuned-out and even physically poisoned to the point they don't care.

We're at the beginning of what the Illuminati are calling 'The Great Reset,' which spells the death of the United States and the transition to the true One World Government of the End via the already-established United Nations.

Most people have no idea the UN is the End times one world government of Biblical prophecy, and it was founded precisely by the Illuminati, who control it to this day.

If just that one rock star or teevee star had come across my first book and then tweeted out a link...dang. Someone tweet my book to Elon Musk!! I'm not kidding!!! If he tweeted out my book the Illuminati would have the biggest challenge ever upon them in the history of the Great Plan: A Mass Awakening of Humanity.

Hopefully, for your sake, you are an _**old**_ friend of mine, who had read my first book and were awake and aware of what the New World Order was cooking when it came time to have ~~an experimental~~ a depopulation vaccine shoved down your throat. Most weren't and this will cost them, and us.

There were no long-term side effect studies of any of the 4 'emergency' covid vaccines. They never operated under FDA approval but instead Emergency Use Authorization (EUA) because "no other accepted treatment was available to treat covid 19", which has been proven to be a huge lie.

Vaccines typically take ten years to develop and must go through phase I, phase II and phase III studies to determine safety, long-term efficacy, and long-term side effects. After the phase III trials and analysis, the drug's scientific-backed clinical trials go to an FDA panel where they analyze the results and make a group-vote on rejection or approval. These extreme safety protocols did not happen with the covid vaccines, leaving people wide open to "possible" long-term side effects.

Again, these 4 vaccines pushed by the criminal stalwarts of Big Pharma have **ZERO** long-term side-effect studies, and most of those injections utilized a brand-new gene-therapy, mRNA. Those who took the mRNA shots are in grave danger now of blood clots, heart attacks and strokes.

The inventor of the mRNA technology, Dr. Robert Malone, has gone public since the release of the mRNA injections by Pfizer and Moderna and stated that people should NOT be taking these injections as they were cytotoxic in the short term, and the long-term effects in humans were unknown.

These vaccines were then administered to 5.4 billion people on the planet, with the highest concentration of vaccine uptake among the 1st world countries' citizens, promoted and pushed by psychopath elites, and often under mandatory conditions by the Illuminati-controlled federal and state governments.

__"If you want to wait and see if a side effect shows up two years later, that takes two years," Bill Gates said. "So, when you're acting quickly… this is a public good, so those trade-offs will be necessary."__

-Head eugenicist and vaccine-pusher "Slow Kill" Bill Gates, referring to the "deadly" pandemic and the new coronavirus vaccines' risk profile a few months before they were released upon the public. Quote from BBC Breakfast, April 2020

And after everyone who could be convinced to take the highly-risky vaccine did, what did Gates have to say about the "deadly" pandemic two years later, on May 5, 2022, while on a book tour?

__"…then, at that point (2020), we didn't really understand that the fatality rate, you know, we didn't understand that it's a FAIRLY LOW__ *fatality rate. And that it's a disease mainly of the elderly, kind of like flu is, although a bit different than that."*

The fact of the matter is the overall survival rate of Covid-19 is north of 99.6%!!!

Throw in a bunch of faulty PCR tests—of which the inventor and Nobel prize winner Cary Mullis said WEREN'T to be used to test for viruses and conveniently died right before the pandemic went off—and a media-scare campaign green-lighted by the controlled feds and paid for by Big Pharma and suddenly everybody wants to be a guinea pig. And their grandparents. And their kids. And their babies. God help us all.

In November 2022 I read statistics listed by Bloomberg regarding the carnage. 12.7 BILLION doses administered, the lion's share of those with the mRNA technology.

5.4 billion humans have at least one shot in them, that's about 70% of the total global population.

613 million injections in the USA, with 80% of the population with at least one injection.

The Georgia Guidestones stipulated that only 500 million people or less should be alive on Earth at any given time. The global population is vastly larger than that, currently 8 billion. 70% have at least one shot in them. 70% off 8 billion is 2.4 billion. We're well on our way as people are dropping dead left and right as this book goes to print in mid 2023… **about two years after the first injections.** Slow-Kill Bill was right…

And coincidentally or not, an odd event happened Summer of 2022 regarding the Georgia Guidestones. You know by now that there are no coincidences in this realm, all pertinent events are completely planned out and executed for the next ones to come.

The Guidestones, which had stood for 40+ years having opened to the public in March 1980, were physically damaged on July 5, 2022 by an "unknown" assailant. Someone detonated a bomb at the site, damaging the stone pillars...allegedly. Two days later, they were demolished completely by whoever oversaw the display and the site closed permanently.

It's almost as if the directions inscribed on the pillars weren't needed any more, the Great Reset was now set into motion to complete the "commandments" literally carved in stone. No more guidance was needed or required, the ship had set sail and humanity had taken the bait and willingly euthanized themselves.

The coming, resulting global infrastructure collapse from this many vaccine-injected people dropping dead suddenly, or being incapacitated and needing care, unable to function and eventually die will whittle the remaining unvaccinated 2.4 billion down dramatically as the system breaks down so I expect the Illuminati will meet their goal of under a 500-million global population with this false-flag-to-end-all-false-flags by their stated timeframe of 2030.

They've got to get rid of all these pesky, carbon-footprinting first-worlders: The citizens of the United States, Europe, Japan, Canada, Australia, and New Zealand. These are the people who most will not want to go willingly and quietly away from their comfortable, first-world lifestyles as the incoming Green Religion commands.

If they don't disappear then their apex-consumer lifestyles will kill the Earth and all who live on it through Climate Change.... or so they say, promote and will soon enforce on what's left of the population come 2030.

Never mind that the people who are orchestrating this massive control-scam all fly around the world in private jets, have thousands of servants, live in huge mansions, and hoard the world's wealth by the hundreds of trillions of dollars.

Since us useless eaters won't bother to save the environment and go willingly to our early graves, there had to be an engineered event to trick us into going on our own for the good of the earth and humanity-at-large.

No, the Federal Government in the United States did not put a gun to your head and tell you to take an injection, but they did everything BUT that to coerce people who didn't want the jab into getting it, plus they were the ones who approved it's use via the FDA.

~~Baal~~ Bill Gates comes from an elite, eugenicist family. His father was head of Planned Parenthood at one time according to Bill himself! He WANTS to depopulate the planet and was probably groomed for exactly the role he played in the plannedemic: Head Depop-Shot-Pusher. Major events going on today were planned out decades ago.

After all, Gates is a big philanthropist who loves and cares about people and only wants to help them, right?

Maybe that's why his name turned up on multiple different flight manifests of pedophile Jeffrey Epstein's "Lolita Express" jet flights to billionaire Epstein's private Caribbean Island loaded with underage runaways, kidnap victims, and even 'farmed' adolescents who were born into sexual bondage through Satanic families.

This is the same Bill Gates who was photographed standing with Jeffrey Epstein and the same Bill Gates who did business with Epstein.

And the same Bill Gates whose wife announced she was divorcing him in May 2021 because of all the above to do with Epstein!

But he's a great guy and he's rich, so surely he's smart and we can trust him, right?

Good-guy Gates donated all his money to a tax-free foundation so the IRS couldn't ever touch it…what a humanitarian!! Then diversified that now-protected-from-tax Microsoft stock into holdings such as Moderna, the other company besides Pfizer offering an mRNA clotshot.

Then humanitarian Gates further diversified into farmland so much that he is now the largest private landowner in the United States. Then he bought hundreds of millions of dollars worth of Monsanto stock to make sure the GMO poisonous food would keep coming on his new farms. And he's such a hero that he tried to vaccinate the entire world against the rages of a deadly pandemic.

What a guy.

Now, I had not even HEARD the term "Great Reset" before the pandemic hit, and that's because the plannedemic was the planned, intentional initiation of the Great Reset.

I had not heard of the people behind the Great Reset either, the World Economic Forum, as they evaded my radar until the pandemic started and they came out of the shadows as the Bilderberg Group-on-steroids.

The WEF is the more-public-friendly, more-inclusive Bilderberg Group basically, the new high-profile face of the Great Plan agenda.

Going forward, the WEF will be the public representative body of the NWO/Illuminati so they are worth keeping a close watch on. Visit their website. Read what they are saying because what they say and want will be our reality coming right up.

Their plan is to convince the general public that this "random" pandemic that we were ill-prepared for, but were warned against by Bill Gates and Dr. Fauci, is the cause of what is coming: Economic Armageddon.

Blaming this on the plannedemic will be a lie. They have planned this Great Reset from the very start, every step of it.

"....A global plan called the Great Reset is underway. Its architect is a global élite that wants to subdue all of humanity, imposing coercive

measures with which to drastically limit individual freedoms and those of entire populations. In several nations this plan has already been approved and financed; in others it is still in an early stage. Behind the world leaders who are the accomplices and executors of this infernal project, there are unscrupulous characters who finance the World Economic Forum and Event 201, promoting their agenda....”

-Archbishop Carlo Maria Vigano, "Open letter to the President of the United States of America Donald J. Trump," October 25, 2020

In October 2019, just weeks before the 'pandemic' hit, the WEF's Event 201 was conducted.

"Event 201: A Global Pandemic Exercise" took place on October 18, 2019.

This was a simulation of a coronavirus (!!!) pandemic that would last for 18 months and kill 65 million people globally.

This was an 18-month simulation crammed into a 3.5-hour presentation that you yourself can watch on YouTube as of the publishing date of this book.

The purpose of this simulation was to try and gauge what would happen to the world and society if a pandemic hit being as unprepared as we were.

They were testing the water to see if the time was right to light the fuse on the Great Reset.

It was.

In July 2020, a mere four months into the pandemic, Head of the WEF, Klaus Schwab, published a book called "Covid 19: The Great Reset". In this book he blames the pandemic for the social and economic woes to come...his public prediction at that time, but in reality this is called "Revelation of the Method" in which the Illuminati put their plans right out there for the sheep to see and it goes right over their heads. A ritual mocking of the victims…us!

If you get a second, read some of the book reviews on Amazon for Schwab's book…people aren't pulling any punches over what the WEF is planning for us!!

In November 2020, less than a year into the plannedemic and one year since Event 201, The Great Reset was featured on the cover of Time Magazine no less to tell the sheep what is coming. They are not hiding it at all but no one even knows about it or that it is well underway.

People are just so distracted with everything that our busy society grinds us through that they don't have time, energy or even the direction to do any research…let alone when a plannedemic is scaring the crap out of them and their families, occupying every worrying moment.

And all of that frightening-crazy chaos, confusion and deception was what led to so many people to blindly and willingly be injected with the covid vaccines.

Most people will take the time to read at least a couple of reviews for any new product they haven't experienced before on Amazon or the like, but if you do any research before getting an experimental jab from literal criminal sources who were granted immunity from liability and you're a conspiracy theorist nutjob.

Pfizer, the largest supplier of the covid vaccines with mRNA tech, had the USA's biggest criminal fine in history levied against it.

On September 2, 2009 the Justice Department announced the largest health care fraud settlement in United States history. Pfizer was ordered to Pay **$2.3 Billion** for fraudulent marketing for a single product, Bextra, that has since been pulled off the shelves ***due to safety concerns*** !!!

That didn't stop Pfizer from promoting it and making profits from it right up until the day they were ordered by the FDA to pull it. Seems like there is still a lot of covid vaccine advertising and promoting going on right this second in the face of growing evidence of massive public harm…hmmmmmmm.

The Illuminati are not going to run us through this gigantic false flag and NOT commit the culling of mankind. If this wasn't the real deal, they would risk having millions or billions of people wake up to the Great Plan for a New World Order.

Millions have woken up since the start of the plannedemic, started looking for the truth about what is happening, started prepping, awakening others, making torches and nooses, sharpening pitchforks, building gallows, etc….or at least they better be dammit!!

People would be too weary and wise to go along with this whole rigamarole again.

The Illuminati only got one kick at the cat and they are moving to quash the United States and First-world humanity over this plannedemic.

Most of the jabs weren't mandatory, the people themselves sought out the injections that never had FDA approval, only Emergency Use Authorization (EUA). Between that and the 1986 Vaccine Injury Act, Pfizer, Moderna and the rest cannot be held responsible for what is happening right this second and to come.

The CDC/FDA/NIH crime bosses publicly stated that they were allowing the experimental vaccines to be rushed through without even animal testing because this is *'such an emergency…the economy and society won't recover unless we immediately eradicate COVID-19'* or whatever BS-excuse they spit out. The CDC even added the covid injections and boosters to the annual vaccine schedule for our kids!!

'Rushing it through for the *good of humani*ty' will be the excuse for not discovering the 'side effect' of extreme injury and/or DEATH that I'm going to show you is showing up right now after these injections.

11

They've never been able to come up with a coronavirus (common cold) vaccine before in history. Why were they able to do it now and so quickly?

Because all the world's a stage and they already had the "vaccine" all ready to go. The pandemic was made for the vaccine, not the other way around.

The Illuminati were smart enough to not put themselves at risk by releasing a highly-dangerous pathogen on the general public because they themselves would be at risk, especially since the controlling body of the modern-day Illuminati are all 'elderly' and most over 60 years old.

Much better for them to use their Big Pharma to convince us we needed to take a vaccine for our protection and then use their controlled media to push that narrative.

You better believe they all were taking Ivermectin and Hydroxychloroquine the whole time as treatments and preventatives, while having their media project the exact opposite: HCQ and especially Ivermectin were harmful to take we were told.

The fact is, Ivermectin is a Nobel-prize-winning wonderdrug and is one of the safest drugs ever invented.

Shutting down HCQ and Ivermectin use led to the problem we're going to go over now...

It seems that since the mass-vaccinations began in late December of 2020, the annual 'excess death rate not counting covid deaths' has been increasing by leaps and bounds in the first-world countries...and no government or globalist corporation that supposedly know all can figure out why. No scientists. No think tanks. Nothing. Nobody can figure out what's wrong. Imagine that.

And if a legitimate doctor or scientist says that the increasing ailments and deaths are from the vaccine they are immediately smothered by the media as crazy or just flat out ignored.

They wanted to get as many jabs into people's arms as possible before the "long term" side effects started to show up and people got smart about things.

We have a major problem that began showing up the last half of 2021 with hundreds of thousands of people suddenly dying who shouldn't have.

The fact that this was reported in social media truth-circles and then smothered by the same social media and the mainstream media is criminal.

There are literally hundreds of thousands of "extra" deaths occurring nationally here in the US and millions globally and the first rounds of jabs given earlier in 2021 are the smoking gun.

In January 2022 the CEO of OneAmerica life insurance, a $100 billion company, said the **national death rate in the USA is up 40% from pre-pandemic** levels for working class people, 18-62 years old.

"We are seeing, right now, the highest death rates we have seen in the history of this business-not just at OneAmerica. The data is consistent across every player in that business...And what we just saw in third quarter (2021), we're seeing it continue into the fourth quarter, is that death rates are up 40% over what they were pre-pandemic...Just to give you an idea of how bad that is, a three-sigma or a one-in-200-year catastrophe would be 10% increase over pre-pandemic so 40% is just unheard of."
-J. Scott Davison, CEO OneAmerica

The fuse was lit when the first shots started going in arms in December 2020, the 'long term' deaths from the shots appear to have started showing up around 6 months after first injections… in third quarter 2021.

There is a sizable and growing list of students and athletes who are dropping dead during games from heart attacks. There are also famous people suddenly dropping dead. You hear about these in the media but not the thousands of useless eaters dying daily.

And the kids…literally the future of humanity. That's the worst part of it all.

Injecting 5 to 11-year-old kids who would have no more risk of dying than a common cold if they were to contract Covid19 is insanity. So, they too were injected with a rushed vaccine with manipulated testing trials and non-existent long-term safety data.

They even currently have babies in clinical trials for the Pfizer vax… these people pushing this forward on naïve humanity will surely burn hot and fast in Hell.

Once the handwriting shows up on the public wall with the long-term side effect profile realized, and the prospects of a horrible future and either a heart attack/stroke at any given moment or a prolonged, agonizing death from autoimmune disease or worse, hundreds or thousands or MILLIONS will have literally nothing to lose by going after those who condemned them by tricking them into taking the clotshots.

They may martyr themselves by the dozens, hundreds, thousands or even millions, physically rallying and attacking those who facilitated the homicidal injections. People like Fauci, Gates and other high-level puppets should be shaking in their boots about now.

Since the Federal Government, and all governments for that matter, are collectively a faceless, impersonal entity comprised of people who are supposed to be acting in our best interests and were put in place by the majority of people…or so it is made to appear…this debacle of 'unforeseen' deadly long-term side effects will be blamed on **us.**

Voting corruption notwithstanding, the blame finger will be pointed squarely at the citizens of the first-world nations for electing a bunch of corrupt idiots who were unprepared for a pandemic.

While they distracted us with professional sportsball, teevee, movies, video games, social media, GMO-foods and other manufactured chaos, we allowed our politicians and thereby governments to be bought off via lobbyists and backroom-deals.

When this whole "plannedemic" went off in early 2020 I had sort of begun working on book 3 of this series, but its title was going to be "Rise of the New World Order 3: Resonance", and it had nothing to do with a pandemic and forced vaccines.

It was going to be about the fantastic technologies of Nikola Tesla that were confiscated when he died in 1943 by the Feds because the technology was too dangerous to have floating around out there and end up in rogue, dangerous hands.

You know as well as I that those ultra-powerful discoveries and technologies that Tesla brought into this world were immediately handed right off to the most dangerous and evil hands on the planet, the Satanic Illuminati cabal.

They've been using Tesla technology against us for years at this point and there are patents for all of it. They are pumping aluminum, barium and worse into the atmosphere, the infamous "chemtrails", and then using the HAARP technology to heat the metals in the sky to create high- or low-pressure systems. They can very easily control the weather around the globe this way, among other amazing things the HAARP tech is capable of.

Then: Enter the plannedemic.

I went into full panic mode. I immediately knew in early 2020 from what was happening that there were compulsory if not mandatory vaccinations on the way and I had to get on top of this situation and warn as many people as I could, especially those who HADN'T read my first book and were sitting ducks for the culling.

The concept for the original book 3 got immediately shelved and I started researching about everything to do with the plannedemic. Then I started putting what I was finding out in "Urgent Status Reports" via eBooks on Amazon, hoping people would be notified through Amazon that I had a new mini-book series out and would get the warning they could share with those who didn't.

So, I inserted into those reports some of the information in this book 3. If you've read my update reports you will recognize some of the content here, just as I said I was going to do.

Although the Great Reset is the main subject of this book, it is not the only one for sure. As with my first book, we're going to touch on more than one piece of the conspiracy puzzle for you to follow up on with your own research.

I'm still fulfilling my mission as a called Sentinel, sounding the alarm to alert humanity about the Great Reset, which they have set in motion to see the Great Plan across the finish line.

CHAPTER 2

THE GREAT PLAN
(UPDATED AND ABRIDGED)

"By this plan we shall direct all mankind. In this manner, and by the simplest means, we shall set in motion and in flames. The occupations must be allotted and contrived, that we may in secret, influence all political transactions ..."

-Adam Weishaupt, founder and mastermind of the Illuminati

The plan Weishaupt was talking about was his own updated version of the 4,000-year-old Great Plan, now empowered by the Rothschild-controlled global banking cartel wealth and their newly formed (sponsored) Illuminated Seers of Bavaria, aka the Illuminati, est. May 1,1776.

Why May 1? Because May 1 is Beltane, an occult holiday which celebrates the Sun god returning, marking the first day of Summer in ancient times.

Return of the Sun god? We know who that is!! It was their intention that they would be the ones to complete the Great Plan.

The Illuminati operate to this day and are the latest incarnation of the ancient occult secret societies that followed King Nimrod's Great Plan right through history and soon to the End.

They have reaped the benefits of being the head Satanists here on Earth and largely own and control everything on this planet.

The trillions in wealth hoarded by the Illuminati funds their underground black ops labs, where clandestine, illegal, immoral, stomach-turning scientific research and experiments are done to help advance the most nefarious components of the Great Plan.

It is my position starting with Book 1 that the Biblical King Nimrod is the Antichrist, especially with the evidence I presented in Book 2, the Awakening. He will be brought back from the dead 4,000 years after the fact using the Illuminati's modern-day DNA technology to rule the world once again, fulfilling the goal of the Great Plan: For mankind to achieve immortality through science.

Nimrod couldn't live to be 4,000 years old to see the Great Plan to completion and that was the point. When he died, the followers of the first occult secret society he set in motion, the Babylonian Mystery Religion, kept a sample of his DNA safe and hidden away knowing someday they could use it to bring him back to life physically, a perfect clone of his physical body. Once his physical body was up and running again, an occult ceremony using the help of Satan himself would free his soul from the chains of the Abyss and be delivered into the new, physical body.

Revelation 17 is then fulfilled:

__"The beast that you saw was, and is not, and is about to come up out of the abyss and go to destruction. And those who live on the earth, whose names have not been written in the Book of Life from the foundation of the world, will wonder when they see the beast, that he was, and is not, and will come."__

–Revelation 17:8

This quote from Revelation is literally saying that the Antichrist was alive at one point before Revelation was given to John, was NOT alive at the time of John's Revelation, but that he would be alive again towards the End.

It would seem that the return of Nimrod to power is near, as the science exists and the Illuminati have virtually achieved all their goals.

Let's see where we are at today under the Great Plan in 2023...

Remember the original goals of the Illuminati hatched in 1776?

1. Abolition of the Monarchy and all ordered government.
2. Abolition of private property.
3. Abolition of inheritance.
4. Abolition of patriotism.
5. Abolition of the family/morality, and communal education for children.
6. Abolition of all religion.

Let's briefly run through their list of objectives, one by one, and see where we are today, nearly 250 years since the Illuminati's founding in 1776.

They overthrew and got rid of all the independent-minded Kings, Queens, Czars, etc. running Europe and Asia from back in their day. The ones that are left, such as the British Royal Family, are fully vested with the Illuminati and are 100% on board with the Great Plan for a New World Order.

Remember how Prince Andrew got tripped up with pedophile Jeffrey Epstein and the Lolita Express recently? And how it all got swept under the carpet and just went away? Yup. In fact, it all seemed to just disappear.

As for eliminating ordered government? No better way to do that than have a hired gang of lobbyists to buy and install the most morally corrupt people around, those who can be bought off and willing to sell their country down the river tomorrow for a payout today.

Lobbying should 100% be ILLEGAL and there should be term limits for Congress creatures but there aren't because then the corrupted system wouldn't work like they need it to. They need long-term puppets for it to work like they want. Look at people like Nancy Pelosi who has been there DECADES who are worth hundreds of millions of dollars on a pittance Congressman salary. Just as many Republicans have sold us down the river, and that's a fact.

All the governments of the WORLD are on the Illuminati payroll including China and Russia. The Illuminati controlled both Russia and China during and after their respected communist revolutions as the Illuminati were the ones who instigated, funded, steered and controlled them…what makes you think they don't control them today? Of course they do, and all the world's a stage, everything choreographed by the Illuminati's hidden hand.

Don't you think Russia's KGB would know about the New World Order and therefore Putin would? He does. I've seen quotes alleged to have come from him about the New World Order and being against it but have found no credible sources. Until he stands on the floor of the UN and calls out the Illuminati I'm going with what the facts show and I therefore logically believe: The Illuminati control it all.

Abolition of private property? That sounds like something called socialism to me.

No wonder they have been promoting socialism in the public-school system so much recently. Tons of Millennials are socialist-minded and Generation Z will be worse, and even worse after that. The number of Millennials who wanted to see Bernie Sanders as President was disturbing to say the least. They just don't understand how socialism really works. It fails. Every time. Miserably.

These are the exact same brainwashed people who will be taking the reins of power someday and it will fall right into place with the agenda of the New World Order as the Great Plan/NWO is a "leftist" and socialist structure of rule under the Antichrist. This is why today, nearing the End, virtually all mainstream media is on the side of the leftist/globalist agenda in order to help promote it, particularly to the younger generations.

The Millennials and Gen Z know their future looks bleak and they bought into the socialism pipe dream hook, line, and sinker. After "capitalism" fails here right quick due to the pyramid-scheme Federal Reserve imploding the dollar, socialism will look even more attractive. All by plan.

Abolition of inheritance? This goes hand-in-hand with abolition of private property. If you don't own anything you have nothing to pass down to your descendants. They want everything you own to be turned over to the state when you die instead of being able to amass wealth, which would be a threat to their power. This was the impetus for the tax-free foundations where the elites house their private wealth to protect it from exactly this.

"Abolition of Patriotism" ....here we go ★★★rolls eyes and sighs★★★...

I personally embrace the values and guidance afforded to us in our Constitution and for what that represents as an idealistic guide I am

100% pro. I enjoy the comradery of my fellow **patriotic** Americans no matter what race, religion, sexual orientation or whatever they are, we are all in this crazy matrix together. It is these points that me proud to be an American on one hand.

On the other?

I'm ashamed, and worse afraid, that I hail from the United States. The USA is the New Babylon of the End times. No single empire has been more corrupt, perverted, and tyrannical than the United States of America. We have run up our country's credit card to the moon and built an empire on the debt we incurred through the Federal Reserve. Money is the god of most in the USA where people's ultimate goal is to become rich, powerful and famous in this life.

We have bombed countries all over the world for the last hundred years yet never have been bombed ourselves. We've been virtually untouchable. That's going to change and soon, as the runaway karma train is coming 'round the bend headed straight for us.

The NWOwned Mainstream Media and public miseducation system is beating it into the sheep that the USA is an evil, racist and tyrannical country and we need to destroy it and start over as socialists...and this will eventually come to pass.

After 9/11, the Military Industrial Complex, owned and controlled by the Illuminati shareholders, had all their Neocon puppets in place when the false flag we know as 9/11 went off.

"We", meaning the USA as a whole--citizens, businesses, and government--invaded Afghanistan and Iraq and bombed them back to the Stone Age, murdering millions over a manufactured lie called 9/11.

The USA is now nearly universally hated worldwide for this and other empire-building exercises, and since most people in the world associate the United States with naïve/entitled white people and white

Christian men especially, you can see how easy it is to work up the 'people of color' against the USA in America today.

Europe is in an interesting spot also with all the 'refugees' that were brought in for what is coming, the manufactured friction between Islam and Christianity that the Antichrist will 'solve', making him the hero that people will follow. This is all preplanned and unfolding right in front of us, the Biblical script executed by the Illuminati.

And now this kneeling business when it comes time to play our National Anthem before we sit down to watch the weekly sportsball bread-and-circus show the elites are still putting on after thousands of years?

Rome burned to the ground because everyone was intentionally distracted while the country went down in flames. By the time the people realized it the barbarians were at the gates and their empire had been dissolved.

History repeats.

We're almost to that point.

Again.

"Abolition of the family, elimination of societal morals and state-indoctrination for the children."

I don't need to tell you of the divorce rate. My childhood was severely and negatively impacted by the divorce of my parents as are millions of others, and that's the plan.

The Baby Boomers, living through the exploding excesses of the 1970s and 80s, felt that having a good time was more important than commitments and responsibilities, and trying to make a marriage work like the old days. At least that was my situation in 1986 when my parents divorced, sending me at 16 years old careening headlong into alcohol and drugs to rebel against anything and everything.

The Tavistock Institute's planned counterculture revolution of the 1960s brought loose sexual morals and ever-more-powerful drugs to the masses.

How about the synthetic opiod epidemic raging through the world right this second, killing thousands and more.

The advent of pornography was surely a harbinger of the End, and now 1000x worse thanks to free online porn that can be accessed by anyone old enough to use a cell phone. We have Tinder and other apps for random, promiscuous sexual hookups. Even gay marriage was recently legalized by the government.

On June 26, 2015 the US Supreme Court legalized gay marriage nationwide. Gay marriage was just the beginning down the road to good ol' Sodom and Gomorrah. Now we've got 'trans kids' running around and we are expected to accept that that is the new societal norm. Now they are pushing for kids who aren't even old enough to decide their bedtime to decide if they want to undergo gender reassignment surgery...this is complete madness.

Never in mankind's history has the world been so completely and utterly in a death grip by the evil ones. Think about it. The family unit never had a chance against a coordinated attack by the Illuminati. Neither did societal morals.

The state-indoctrination kicked into overdrive with the advent of "Common Core". The result is that we have two generations of vaccine-damaged, fluoridated, medicated, and confused kids who hate the United States and think that their only future rests with global socialism. Ugh.

Lastly, 'Abolition of religion,' or at least all of the different religions in favor of the one world religion, the worship (again) of King Nimrod/the Antichrist.

Hmmm....seems that during the pandemic lockdowns the local governments largely shut down all churches in the name of 'public safety' but you could still go to the store and buy liquor, weed, junk food, etc. but ohhhhh-nooooooo it's not safe to go to church for an hour once a week under your own free will.

There were even parishioners and clergy ARRESTED and put in JAIL, where there was plenty of room because the local gooberments let out scot-free thousands of prisoners "for their safety during a pandemic" to make room for the religious and patriotic!!!

I would say that the Illuminati were successful in the endeavor of their line-item goals. They've got us on the ropes. We're in big trouble, folks.

CHAPTER 3

STATE OF THE STATE

As I'm working through the construction of this book, there are any number of significant events happening around the world, most of them happening under Illuminati influence as they steer us towards the End.

Firstly, going forward, they needed a corrupt and compromised man to take over the White House in order to do the Illuminati's bidding and get the Great Plan back on track. Trump was not the guy for the job, at least it didn't appear that way, so all strings were pulled to get Biden in and, yes, I believe the election was rigged for Biden.

Those who seem to be friends with the United States one week are enemies the next if it suits the Great Plan. I'm talking about the Russians and their "invasion" of Ukraine.

The Ukraine conflict will soon be accompanied by a China-Taiwan conflict and will probably escalate to WWIII status. This should happen AFTER the financial crash, so beware. It is then that the United States will finally feel the sting of foreign conflicts coming to our doorstep, whereby the conflicts of the past were largely contained to Europe/Asia/Africa.

Our comeuppance will arguably arrive in the form of an EMP, either from a nuclear device or from employing the terrifying technological power of Tesla's HAARP technology, of which Russia and China also possess. I've studied HAARP intently and I believe they could use it to

EMP us without a single missile fired = no warning and no chance to shoot it out of the sky.

Europe/NATO will probably also be EMP'd to finish off Western Civilization for good and usher in the new 'global civilization' under the UN....kind of like a 'reset' or something (!)

Between now and then you can expect a banking collapse accompanied by a Wall Street, real estate/housing, and dollar collapse.

We've got a bumpy ride ahead in other words.

CHAPTER 3A

2020 SELECTION

"If the American people ever allow private banks (the Federal Reserve) to control the issue of their currency, first by inflation, then by deflation, the banks and corporations that will grow up around them will deprive the people of all property until their children wake up homeless on the continent their Fathers conquered...."
-Thomas Jefferson, 3rd US President and one of the Founding Fathers

"Bad men cannot make good citizens. It is impossible that a nation of infidels or idolaters should be a nation of freemen. It is when a people forget God that tyrants forge their chains. A vitiated state of morals, a corrupted public conscience, is incompatible with freedom"
-Patrick Henry, one of the Founding Fathers

Corruption rules our country's government from top to bottom and an honest politician is virtually unheard of. Nobody personalized this recently more than Ron Paul, and this is why he was torn apart as a mad-raving lunatic when he made waves going into the 2008 Presidential election.

If Paul would have gained traction and gotten in he would have moved immediately to eliminate the Federal Reserve and put the power of money back into the hands of the American public as the Constitution states it legally must be to prevent exactly what has happened to us.

Since it's been put into motion and we're at the very beginning stages of the Great Reset, there is no way that the Illuminati were going to stand to have Trump in the way setting their timetable back. Everything is supposed to happen and be 'reset' by the year 2030 according to their timetable, that's 7 years from now and it's going to be a crazy 7 years. The whole system must be obliterated including the United States as a country and brought fully under UN control by 2030.

They gave us a particular year to have it in place before. Remember Agenda (20)21? That was just another one of their "excercises" that happens before events like 9/11 and the plannededmic. They knew they would not be able to pull off that target date but wanted to see how the public would react to having the notion of manmade climate change shoved down their throat by the United Nations.

The silence from general humanity about it is largely deafening, somewhat depressing, and downright ominous. Most people are pretty oblivious to it so onward they shall steamroller over us all.

They need all their incompetent and corrupt puppets in place for this and not an apparent outsider like Trump. Trump is certainly a smart guy and a successful businessman despite what is said in the media, and not a creature of DC.

I still don't know for sure whether or not Trump is controlled opposition and works for them, especially after Operation Warp Speed, and then promoting that he was the one who got the covid vaccines to the people. I do believe Trump knows about the NWO, Illuminati, illegal Federal Reserve, etc., but he also knows why JFK was assassinated. I think he is opposed to them and their agenda at heart, at least, whether they are blackmailing him or not.

I give him the benefit of the doubt though, because I read one of Trump's books right after I graduated in 1988, The Art of the Deal, that came out in 1987. In it, he calls out the pedophilia of the elite, including naming Merv Griffin and Malcolm Forbes in particular as gay pedophiles who regularly solicited underage male prostitutes. This was disgusting and reprehensible according to Trump in his book.

I do believe Trump loves our country and pushed the line as far as he could without risking being killed, including having to go along with this vaccine business...or else. This is why the Illuminati underlings took it out on him publicly, trying to impeach him twice. This is unheard of. This is while Joe Biden and his son Hunter walk free while there is enough evidence on the Hunter Biden laptop to put them both away for life.

This is a prime example of Illuminati-enabled corruption at the very top of the political power pyramid. These people are untouchable, and Hunter Biden was dumb enough to document this capstone-level corruption with physical proof and the FBI shut it all down. Facebook and Twitter buried it on social media, the entire reason they are there is to control the narrative and keep the Great Plan on track.

So we all know the puppets are corrupt, but how are they elected repeatedly time and again, people like the Clintons, who are literally career criminals?

Let's briefly revisit a section from my first book, 2013's The Culling of Man:

...Let's start off with the people who we "elected" to drive our country straight into the ground....

Campaign donations and clandestine actions from pro-New World Order entities aside, we've got a terrible issue we need to address, and that is a legitimate, factual concern about voting machine fraud.

The proponents of the Great Plan have pulled out all the stops to advance their agenda, and have left no avenue uncompromised to complete their mission.

Think about this: The 50 states in the USA are divided into over 3,000 counties. Ohio, for instance, is divided into 88 counties, Iowa is divided into 99 counties, and so on. In approximately 1% of these counties, there are paper ballots which are hand counted properly, the way all of our counties should be counting our ballots. This respectable 1% consists of about half of the counties in New Hampshire---the "Live Free or Die" state---and a very few, very small counties scattered throughout the rest of the United States.

In 99% of the other compromised counties, the Democratic and Republican controlled Boards of Elections make sure that the ballots are commandeered from the neighborhood precincts as the polls close their doors. This is to make sure that the neighborhood citizens and other watchdog-patriots do NOT have a chance to count, or at least spot-check, their own votes.

Such counting or spot-checking by the citizens would make centralized computer vote-rigging impossible. This is why the Illuminati, who today control both the national Democratic and Republican parties through the CFR, vehemently oppose any such citizen participation at the neighborhood precinct level. This is because centralized counting is the common feature of all governments trying to rig elections.

In these 99% of USA counties, citizens are forced to use either computer or machine methods of casting a ballot. Vote counting is wide open for fraud this way. The Democratic and Republican parties at the county level delegate the "counting" to one of a small handful of privately-

owned companies which count 99% of the votes in United States national elections in complete secret, with no independent verification or audit.

Currently the four companies which are delegated the power to count the votes in the USA were Election Systems & Software, Diebold, Hart, and Sequoia.

The local county election boards use armed guards to make sure the citizens, candidates, and reporters cannot see what these private companies are doing to the ballots in the "counting room" on election night.

Since 1973, the powers behind the RNC and the DNC have arm-twisted, persuaded, and bullied the local governments in most counties in the USA to unconstitutionally delegate the vote counting to these four mysterious companies. By 1988, the counting companies had consolidated their control over 49 states, and half of New Hampshire.

The private companies controlling the ballots are given a direct feed to a team of manipulators which represent a pool of the AP wire service and the major TV Networks, all under Illuminati control.

The vote-fraud cartel was further empowered through the implementation of the criminal "Help Americans Vote Act" of 2002 or HAVA, which should really be called the "Helping the New World Order by Computer Fraud" Act.

HAVA appropriated $4 billion of our money to entice the state and county election offices to implement computer "vote-counting" systems from basically three major companies, Diebold, Sequoia, and Election Systems & Software. These systems provide for no paper trail and no citizen checks and balances. Most people have no idea how their vote is counted, and I'm here to tell you as of right now under this system, your vote doesn't count.

The patriotic organization "Citizens for a Fair Vote Count" has estimated that it would take no more than $400 million dollars per election to hand count every vote on every ballot in the United States. Because *the New World Order proponents and their Mainstream Media insist on easily rigged elections, all you hear is how we can't possibly afford the expense of a hand count.*

We spend hundreds of BILLIONS of dollars supporting our world military empire. Billions of dollars were just spent on just the promotion and advertising for the 2012 Presidential election alone. Why would billions of dollars be spent for a job that only pays $400,000 year unless someone else besides the President is going to benefit? You already know the answer to that.

We can easily fund an honest and accountable vote-counting system by the people, for the people; to ensure that who we want running the country is who gets into power. This is the only way we are going to get our foot in the door and get some real "change" in this country.

So, in a nutshell, it's either paper ballots/hand counting for an honest election and real change, or corrupted centralized computer counting by the proponents of the New World Order and the usual suspects stay in office...over and over and over, pushing our country further and further under water.

Which would you prefer?

People wanted change so bad they held up their noses at pinnacle-of-corruption-puppet Hillary Clinton and so many people voted for Trump that even the corrupted voting system was overwhelmed and he got in.

Does anyone even remember Hillary and a host of other elite Democrats protesting the 2016 election results, saying it was rigged? They expected a rigged win...for THEM! If that's not the kettle calling the pot black, I don't know what is!!

Trump got in and started making policy decisions with a patriotic **nationalist** outlook, which is good for the citizens of the United States because that means that he put us first, and the rest of the world second. Literally, Make America Great Again and started us on the path to righting our ship....it seemed.

Nationalist Trump pulled us out of the treasonous Paris Climate Accord and Trans Pacific Partnership/TPP also, which Biden promptly signed us back up for both immediately upon taking the reins.

When Trump left office we were fully energy independent, even exporting the extra we didn't need! What did Biden do? The exact opposite and now we're beholden to hostile foreign interests once again. The first day in office, January 20, 2021, Biden shut down the Keystone pipeline!!!

Trump's actions across the board resulted in having one of the best economies EVER **with record high Black and Latino employment**---everybody was working and doing great. Patriotism was surging too.

That is not how the globalists wanted things for the USA as we are scheduled to be terminated, so they initiated the Great Reset, corrupted the 2020 election to the max and got Trump out.

I've seen Lindell's and D'Souza's documentary videos among others about the election corruption and there's no doubt in my mind the election was stolen from Trump and handed right to the intentionally incompetent puppet Biden.

Even FOX news showed their true NWO colors and went against Trump which isn't a surprise since the guy calling the shots at FOX, James Murdoch, son of Rupert Murdoch, gave the Biden campaign $1.5 million!!

You can search for the tweets of ultra-leftist James' wife crowing about how they helped beat Trump on Twitter! If you're not done with FOX you better be because in the end it's all pro-NWO.

Even before the election was finalized, the bought-and-paid-for media crowned Biden the President with no authority to do so and unconditionally sold it to the nation that Biden won, that there was no voter fraud, and that he was to be sworn in January 2021…and to celebrate and rejoice because finally orange man gone.

I don't know what to make of all the Sidney Powell/Linn Wood statements. Where was the "Kraken" they were crowing about? Not a thing Linn Wood said was going to happen did. It was a complete S-show from the get-go so it was just more smoke and mirrors from controlled opposition IMO. And on that note…

Did Trump try to eliminate the Federal Reserve?

Nope.

Did Trump initiate a new 9/11 investigation by a truly independent agency?

No.

Anything become of the Hunter Biden laptop?

Negative.

Was Hillary arrested?

Ha!

Did Trump re-authorize the traitorous NDAA against us, stripping all rights from the general public of the United States of America?

Yes, he did.

Did Trump push hazardous, experimental vaccines with no long-term studies on an unsuspecting public in the name of saving the economy and his reputation?

That's a big YES there.

The fact is that the number one thing Trump could have done to MAGA would have been to eliminate the Federal Reserve and take the money power back from the Illuminati and put it back in the hands of the Congress as it dictates in the Constitution. This was the foundation of Ron Paul's Presidential platform!

Article 1, Section 8, Clause 5 of the United States Constitution:

[The Congress shall have Power . . .] To coin Money, regulate the Value thereof, and of foreign Coin, and fix the Standard of Weights and Measures; . . .

With Trump out of the driver's seat, the mainstream media will now, instead of bashing Trump 24/7, switch over to full-out pushing the NWO-agenda with man-made Climate Change at the top of the talking head's parrot-list.

The political left literally morphed into the party of the New World Order during the plannedemic and will remain so until the End as the Great Plan calls for a leftist/socialist one world order.

In the 1960s the left was all anti-government, anti-censorship, anti-war, full of hippie-love for their fellow man, etc. Now they are exactly the opposite of all that. The left and right have literally switched positions since then. Just shows how controlled the whole thing is and how powerful the media is.

CHAPTER 3B

THE ECONOMY

I'm not an economist or investment advisor other than telling you to buy all the ammo you can get your hands on, but once you are awake and know who's steering our financial ship your guard tends to go up.

By inflating the economy faster and bigger than it would otherwise be by flooding the economy with money (low interest rates), and then taking money back out of the economy (high interest rates) the stock market artificially surges and then falls.

Since the Illuminati know in advance the actions of the Federal Reserve and other global central banks, since it is they who own the central banks and set the interest rates, they can make decisions knowing what will happen in the future. By this, they continually fleece the public by using the stock market in particular. Add to that the power of suggestion by the controlled media on a naïve, unsuspecting public and these ups and downs are further exaggerated and leveraged.

Remember how Nathan Rothschild fooled the British stock traders, looking all sad like he was going to lose his money? Then started dumping his stocks, triggering other investors into a panic and causing them to sell off their stock shares. While this was going on, Rothschild's agents bought up all the panicked investors stocks for pennies on the pound, essentially buying up Great Britain.

The power of suggestion.

Well now they have the mainstream media to fool the people in an even more grandiose way. Think of the "War of the Worlds" broadcast in the 1930s and what happened to public sentiment: UTTER PANIC. And now we have computer-actuated derivatives and shorting of stock on top of all that, which I can't believe either are allowed by the bought-and-paid-for SEC, but it's reality going into the End.

"Compound interest is the eighth wonder of the world. He who understands it, earns it; he who doesn't, pays it."
-Albert Einstein

The people who run the Great Plan, the Rothschild-led Illuminati, have **ALSO** been drawing compounding interest on their money for hundreds of years at this point by owning and controlling the central banks of the world.

They are constantly adding to the amount of money in circulation (inflation) when the federal governments of the world borrow money and then spend it, with reckless spending highly encouraged on things like wars that the Illuminati start and steer. A huge portion of the annual budgets of nations gets flushed down the toilet into the waiting arms of the weapons corporations that the Illuminati also majority-own through stock holdings.

Remember, we are under the ancient occult moneylender scam of fiat currency with additional state-sanctioned fractional reserve lending in place.

The Founding Fathers were well aware of the existence of the ancient money scam of charging interest on money created out of thin air, and the Illuminati and their intentions to implement this system in the new USA through a privately-owned central bank.

The Federal Reserve was founded in 1913, we were told, to control inflation and to stabilize the money and stock markets, which at the time were being roiled intentionally by the Illuminati to sell this Constitutionally-illegal act! This is how they sold it the American public before and after they swindled it into place.

Of course, the installation of the privately-owned, for-profit Federal Reserve had exactly the opposite effect of how it was promoted, by design, and the people just accepted it. They were either unaware of the consequences of this action, or they didn't have the backbone to speak up, save a small handful of patriotic Congressmen who sounded off at the time.

Contrary to their public mission statement, since 1913 the Fed has inflated the money supply so much, that in terms of consumer purchasing power, it would take about three thousand dollars today to purchase what one hundred dollars would in 1913.

The end result of this pyramid scheme once the wheels start to come off is rapid hyperinflation into oblivion, which is largely an overheating and breakdown of the fiat money system coupled with public panic.

As people rush to turn their money into physical assets, THAT will add further fuel to the inflationary conditions as people bid up the prices of physical assets just to get their hands on something before they are left with nothing.

There is just so much money flying around and multiplying to dizzying numbers on a computer monitor in cyberspace that physical mankind simply can't keep up in terms of the money just required to operate and live, which is why it's harder and harder to make it in the world today.

According to truthinaccounting.org, the current "official" National Debt is north of $30 trillion. The real and actual debt owed by the feds is about **$145 trillion** and includes things such as future social security and Medicare payments as the feds already blew all the money taken in for those programs. These two line-items alone come to nearly $100 trillion. That's over $900 thousand per taxpayer we are on the hook for right this second...plus compounding interest.

These numbers are staggering and will only be going up with more deficit spending. Add in exactly the rate of inflation and of course accompanying compounding interest to $145 trillion, oh, and the reckless spending, and you can see why I'm just a tad concerned about our country's financial situation because what they are doing is untenable.

"You'll own nothing...and be happy about it."

-Klaus Schwab, WEF/World Economic Forum Head Vampire in 2016 at the annual Davos Summit, predicting life for humans in the year 2030

When the coming global economic/currency crisis hits for real... the talking heads on the teevee will scapegoat the pandemic and an inept Federal Government and NOT the central bankers with their fiat currencies and fraction-reserve lending that allowed the system to grow out of control but the Illuminati will be the REAL REASON the global economic structure collapsed...and the Illuminati will be off Scot-free with their ill-gotten planet Earth and everything on it.

Multi-billionaires like Mark Zuckerberg, Bill Gates, Jeff Bezos, the founders of Google, etc., are all-in for the United Nations as the one world government. All of them or their immediate underlings regularly attend United Nations/Bilderberg/CFR/WEF meetings, etc. Remember, money is power. Gates and Bezos have billions. The Illuminati families who run the Great Plan are worth in the hundreds of trillions. Bill Gates is a piker compared to a Rothschild or Rockefeller.

The Illuminati have used this monopoly money to buy up real, physical assets that WON'T disappear like the digital money so many hold in the stock market via their life savings and retirement accounts.

They also have in their physical possession virtually all the mined gold in the world, majority holdings in all the international corporations, real estate, property and land, expensive art and jewelry, etc. All of it physical assets, all of it ill-gotten.

You heap onto our financial system everything above and then add in the existence of derivatives and also shorting of stocks and there's no way the money system CAN'T fail.

Derivatives are basically bets (options) placed on bets placed on even more bets. Just contracts that move money around. Has nothing at all to do with buying a company's stock to support it and maybe get a dividend, which was the purpose of issuing stock to start with. Now the pirates are fully in charge and derivatives are used to manipulate the markets and skim off billions in monopoly money.

And shorting a stock is just as bad if not worse to the people who are in the stock market for honorable and honest reasons. When you short a stock you are allowed to borrow a share of that stock from a broker, sell it into the market as if you own it, and then after a certain time period you buy it back, hoping the price went down. You pocket the difference, minus the broker fee. The kicker is, by selling the stock you borrowed to start with you are automatically helping to trend the stock's price down, a self-fulfilling prophecy. When you do this on large scale you can cause panic selling, make millions and billions of dollars, and ruin companies this way and many have exactly done this, and it's all legal.

All they have to do is go big on shorting the market, which will in itself cause a mini-crash, then use their owned-and-controlled mainstream media to get a panic going and then short it right into the ground. The crash. And the Illuminati will make money all the way to the bottom through their shorting of stock.

People get lulled into complacency when they see the stock market going up. It's when it starts to go down by leaps and bounds that people are suddenly interested in their money.

Do you ever wonder why they stop the stock market when it starts to drop precipitously, by one or two thousand points at a time, but won't do the same when it goes up? Investors have what are called 'stops' in place, and they are automatic/computerized sell orders as opposed to calling up your stock broker and telling him to sell if you're losing too much money. It is done automatically, in microseconds, at a certain number by computer.

The problem is, so many people have these in place, once they start to trigger on the way down it causes the market to drop as entire portfolios of stocks are sold to fulfill the stop order. This causes the market to drop further, which triggers more stop orders, which causes the market to drop even further, which triggers more stops until the whole thing would chase its way down to zero if they didn't stop the bleeding in order to let everyone calm down.

Coming right up, I would hazard a guess that when they stop the stock market 3 or 4 days in a row from dropping, look out below because that is when we are going over the financial cliff.

The same people who set up the central bank pyramid scheme are the same ones who are setting up the new global currency system for after the crash. We're going digital people. RFID chipping of the population is right around the corner and has been practiced for many years at this point already. We are ever-closer to checking off the "Mark of the Beast" box on your End Times bingo card.

The Federal Reserve has been talking about moving to a digital dollar and eliminating cash altogether. As the money-supplier for the United

States they can do whatever they want, they are above the Congress and President, and above the law. This will make upping the money supply much easier than printing billions of paper dollars like the old days when third-world nations descended into hyperinflation, requiring wheelbarrows full of cash to buy a loaf of bread, and then subsequently collapsed.

Don't worry, everyone will have a Federal Reserve wallet being issued to them and the Fed factually will begin issuing 'digital currency' at some point…not that that's all it's been doing since its inception in 1913 creating our money out of thin air!!

Look into SB3571, the Banking for All Act, because that is coming right up and has legislation related to your upcoming personal digital Federal Reserve Wallet which will control your new digital money and of course will track all transactions. And if they don't like what you're doing, they will suspend your account and you won't have any money to do anything.

The end game of everything that is going on is that we are heading into a social credit system just like China has. All your financial info, your medical records/*jab* records, work/family info, all the AI facial-recognition photos and video of you in public, and everything else to do with you is all stored together in a central database and you will receive a societal rating based on the sum total of all of this. The higher the rating means the more subservient you are to the state = the more liberties you are allowed to have.

If you protest on social media or otherwise don't agree with what the Illuminati are doing, you will be struck down to persona non grata.

China has been the model all along. The Rockefellers brought Communism to China in the 1950s and have controlled China ever since. They did this to cultivate and perfect this particular system, now they want it worldwide through the UN.

Only a world government can save us from ourselves, or so we'll be told.

CHAPTER 3C

THE BALANCE

And I don't mean "balance" by equilibrium, I'm talking rounding up some of the miscellaneous events as of late!

Just another harbinger with all this media-suppressed sex-stuff that came to light about Jeffrey Epstein and his personal Boeing 727 "party jet" known popularly among the elites as the Lolita Express, flying nonstop to Epstein's private island in the US Virgin Islands.

I've seen the flight manifest list of who's been there. Tons of Hollywood and political figures, mostly leftists. They just got caught doing what elites and our rulers have been doing since the days of Nimrod, and that's engage in pedophilia.

I'm into fair play and the DC right-wing has had their pedo-issues also. Look up the disturbing tale of "Boys Town"…it's as bad or worse than Epstein's situation.

After you review Boys Town, I think we can agree that a disturbingly high number of celebrities and politicians are actual practicing pedo-Satanists.

Since we're nearing the End, the elites feel they have to hide their true selves less and less. This is now openly manifesting itself yearly at the Super Bowl Halftime Show and the Grammy Awards show in case you haven't been paying attention.

And how about all the trans-kids suddenly? That's what happens when you inject male DNA into females and vice-versa when they are getting all those vaccines as children. Throw in some social-conditioning-brainwashing and viola, you suddenly have thousands or more gender-confused kids.

And of course there's the drag queens who feel the need to interact with children at the local library. And now there's Pride Month, June, to celebrate sodomy with parades and kids and drag queens oh my! We're not in Kansas anymore, Toto.

According to the book of Daniel, the Antichrist is a homosexual. I do believe that all male members of the Illuminati both past and present have engaged in homosexual acts as they are integral parts of both secret society oaths and Satanic ceremonies.

They might not be gay, but they've done gay acts to put it straight (!).

This is why Aleister Crowley was a homosexual, or at least engaged in a lot of…yeah.

All of this spilling out into the open is about grooming and indoctrination.

The thing about true Sodomites is, they largely don't reproduce because of who they're having sex with and the acts themselves. What's happening today is called recruiting, and is about gaining a bigger pool of people to sodomize going forward, and also to increase their numbers for societal power.

CHAPTER 4

THE GREAT RESET
OF HUMANITY

"**The more nationalism and isolationism pervade the global polity, the greater the chance that global governance loses its relevance and becomes ineffective. Sadly, we are now at this critical juncture. Put bluntly, we live in a world in which nobody is really in charge. COVID-19 has reminded us that the biggest problems we face are global in nature. Whether it's pandemics, climate change, terrorism or international trade, all are global issues that we can only address, and whose risks can only be mitigated, in a collective fashion.**"

– Klaus Schwab, Founder and Head of the World Economic Forum, from his 2020 book "COVID-19: The Great Reset"

You may or may not have heard about the **"Great Reset"** before picking up this book.

Although it was on the cover of Time magazine and there are multiple articles there about it, general concern over the Great Reset is largely deferred to as conspiracy theory in the mainstream media.

They know most of the sheep don't really pay attention, aren't awake, and if they try to understand it just goes right over their heads because they don't understand the implications of how evil the people at the WEF are as they are minions of the Illuminati.

It's the rich and powerful unelected that rule the world. The elected are the incompetent, corruptible puppets that execute the will of the unelected, but the media spins it as if the ongoing agenda towards more UN power is coming from the politicians, representing their constituents wishes. This is where this climate-change-business is headed. The talking heads on mainstream media are parroting daily now about being doomed from climate change if we don't reign mankind in.

The real problem is pollution of our environment here on the ground, not miles in the air like the UN would have everyone believe.

This pollution was caused to start with by the Illuminati corporations, profiting from the ecological destruction of the planet as their national businesses turned into multinational corporations.

Just as an example, there is ROUNDUP herbicide in virtually everything we eat up and down the food chain.

That's just one of thousands of examples. They abused the world on all fronts over the last 4,000 years and now they're going to make us pay to "fix it" and enslave us over it.

On July 9, 2020, only 6 months into the 'pandemic', Klaus Schwab published his book "Covid-19: The Great Reset".

The book details how the pandemic will ultimately lead to a crash of the 'system' and will necessitate that out of the ashes will arise a whole new world (order).

According to the WEF:

The Great Reset promises to bring about *"a more secure, more equal, and more stable world"* if everyone on the planet agrees *to "act jointly and swiftly to revamp all aspects of our societies and economies, from education to social contracts and working conditions."*

Allow me to translate from NWO-speak to what Schwab's words **REALLY** mean to you and me: *"The Great Reset promises a global police state, with global socialism for all after the ultimate economic crash of all time and subsequent starvation from the pandemonium, giving way to what's left of humanity alive that didn't starve after the economic crash or die from the mRNA vaccines surrendering their lives and will to the UN as the new, all-powerful global government"*

This is why the public schools, particularly lately in the USA, have been pushing extreme leftism and socialism as trendy and cool.

And it worked. And it WILL be the new system unfortunately.

We now have two generations in the USA, Millennials/Gen Y and Zoomers/Gen Z, who have been brainwashed to be majority pro-NWO and they don't even know it.

As the third generation of brainwashed youth come to voting age, which is called **"Generation Alpha,"** this mindset is going to overwhelmingly show up at the polls and vote for the NWO agenda. This will legitimately put the majority of the people behind it to back the New World Order.

The "New" world order will rise out of the ashes of the Great Reset. The term "world order" denominates a pecking order in the world. Right now, the USA and China are vying for the top spot but all that's going to go away as only the United Nations will remain standing after the dust settles.

When the proponents of the Great Plan/NWO installed the Federal Reserve System as our nation's money supply in 1913 they set the clock in motion to our country's demise.

The end result of the Federal Reserve ponzi scheme---and global fiat money ponzi scheme as the Illuminati owns and controls nearly all global central banks---is the complete destruction of the value of the money, which they've been chipping away at *since inception* by inflating the money supply at will.

If you have time, I HIGHLY suggest you obtain a copy of G. Edward Griffin's classic about the Federal Reserve, money policy, and the great crash that is coming. It is called "The Creature from Jekyll Island" and it is highly reviewed and ranked. It should be in ever researcher's library in paper form because the internet will soon be sterilized of anything to do with exposing the New World Order. This is why I also highly recommend a paper copy of at least my first book as a record of what has happened, and where we're headed.

Now, it is a documented FACT that Bill Gates and Anthony Fauci have been beating the drum of an imminent pandemic for about a decade. A deadly pandemic only comes around every 100 years-ish, so how could they have known, hmmmmmmmmm???

The warnings issued by those in the know before and after the plannedemic tip their hand, they knew this was coming because they had a hand in planning and executing it.

Let's start with Anthony Fauci. You tell me how it's even believable that someone could issue an imminent warning for a 'surprise' outbreak of pandemic??? Are you kidding me!!!

"If there's one message that I want to leave with you today based on my experience, it is that there is no question that there will be a challenge to the coming administration (Trump) in the arena of infectious diseases.... No matter what, history has told us definitively that [outbreaks] will happen," he said. "It is a perpetual challenge. It is not going to go away. The thing we're extraordinarily confident about is that we are going to see this in the next few years.... The mistake that so many people have made ... is a failure to look beyond our own borders in the issue of the globality of health issues, not only things that are there that will come

here but surprises that we'll have... We will definitely get surprised in the next few years"

-Dr. Anthony Fauci, speaking in 2017 at the "Pandemic Preparedness in the Next Administration" at the Georgetown University Medical Center just a few days before Trump was sworn in, January 2017.

Now on to Bill Gates...

Gates has been warning the world about a dangerous pandemic since 2010. Has he been hounding the federal government since then to prepare? No. It's been all lip service, just a casual comment here and there about getting prepared so he could say 'I told you so.'

If I was Gates, I would have held multiple high-level meetings and pounded the point home that we weren't ready and to get prepared, but no, he instead has spent his billions for after-the-fact treatments, aka vaccines. That's where the money's at, not trying to head off a disaster as an ounce of prevention is worth much less than a pound of cure in this case.

The H1N1 flu strain got a lot of attention in 2009. Most of the headlines made it sound dangerous. Early in the epidemic we thought that a very high percentage of infected people were getting sick, and it was quite scary.

But the real story isn't how bad H1N1 was. The real story is that we are lucky it wasn't worse because we were almost completely unprepared for it.

When an epidemic breaks out, there are four steps to try to contain it. The first is to gather data about the disease—where it is and how it is spreading. Second is to limit the movement of people from place to place—with quarantine a last option. Once a disease is widespread this is very hard to do. Third is to have drugs of some type that reduce how much someone infects others and that reduces the severity of the sickness. Fourth is to make a vaccine that is effective against the disease and give it to anyone who is at risk.

We did a reasonable job of gathering data, partly due to the capacity that had been set up to track avian flu. But for all the other steps, we didn't manage to do anything that would have stopped a serious epidemic. In other words, the modest death toll from this flu epidemic is entirely because we were lucky.

Hopefully this outbreak will serve as a wakeup call to get us to invest in better capabilities, because more epidemics will come in the decades ahead and there is no guarantee we will be lucky next time....

– 'A Better Response to the Next Pandemic,' from Gates' personal blog, January 19, 2010

Gates knows how long a vaccine takes to invent and get past the FDA approval process. He is talking here like the vaccine for the upcoming pandemic will be able to roll right out and save the day immediately... strange how he knew how this was going to pan out.

Now this from his 2015 TED speech, titled **'The Next Outbreak? We're not ready"**:

"...So next time, we might not be so lucky (talking about the Ebola outbreak in 2014). You can have a virus where people feel well enough while they're infectious that they get on a plane or they go to a market. The source of the virus could be a natural epidemic like Ebola, or it could be bioterrorism.

So there are things that would literally make things a thousand times worse...But in fact, we can build a really good response system. We have the benefits of all the science and technology that we talk about here.

We've got cell phones to get information from the public and get information out to them.

We have satellite maps where we can see where people are and where they're moving.

We have advances in biology that should dramatically change the turnaround time to look at a pathogen and be able to make drugs and vaccines that fit for that pathogen...

We need to do simulations, germ games, not war games, so that we see where the holes are. The last time a germ game was done in the United States was back in 2001, and it didn't go so well.

So far the score is germs: 1, people: 0...

Now I don't have an exact budget for what this would cost, but I'm quite sure it's very modest compared to the potential harm.

The World Bank estimates that if we have a worldwide flu epidemic, global wealth will go down by over three trillion dollars and we'd have millions and millions of deaths...

There's no need to panic. We don't have to hoard cans of spaghetti or go down into the basement. But we need to get going, because time is not on our side..."

Now from 2016, the BBC interview with "Slow Kill" Bill...

"There's a lot of discussion right now about how we respond in an emergency, how we make sure that the regulatory and liability and organizational boundaries don't slow us down there, so I cross my fingers all the time that some epidemic like a big flu doesn't come along in the next 10 years"

This from a CBS news interview in 2017 at the 2017 World Economic Forum(!) in Davos, Switzerland:

"The impact of a huge epidemic, like a flu epidemic, would be phenomenal because <u>all the supply chains would break down</u>. There'd be a lot of panic. Many of our systems would be overloaded, but being ready for epidemics of different sizes, there's a lot more we should do."

Also in 2017, at the Munich Security Conference in Munich, Germany:

"…When I decided 20 years ago to make global health the focus of my philanthropic work, I didn't imagine that I'd be speaking at a conference on international security policy. But I'm here today because I believe our worlds are more tightly linked than most people realize…

It's also true that the next epidemic could originate on the computer screen of a terrorist intent on using genetic engineering to create a synthetic version of the smallpox virus . . . or a super contagious and deadly strain of the flu.

The point is, we ignore the link between health security and international security at our peril.

Whether it occurs by a quirk of nature or at the hand of a terrorist, epidemiologists say a fast-moving airborne pathogen could kill more than 30 million people in less than a year. And they say there is a reasonable probability the world will experience such an outbreak in the next 10-15 years.

It's hard to get your mind around a catastrophe of that scale, but it happened not that long ago. In 1918, a particularly virulent and deadly strain of flu killed between 50 million and 100 million people.

You might be wondering how likely these doomsday scenarios really are. The fact that a deadly global pandemic has not occurred in recent history shouldn't be mistaken for evidence that a deadly pandemic will not occur in the future.

And even if the next pandemic isn't on the scale of the 1918 flu, we would be wise to consider the social and economic turmoil that might ensue if something like Ebola made its way into a lot of major urban centers. We were lucky that the last Ebola outbreak was contained before it did.

The good news is that with advances in biotechnology, new vaccines and drugs can help prevent epidemics from spreading out of control. And, most of the things we need to do to protect against a naturally occurring pandemic are the same things we must prepare for an intentional biological attack.

First and most importantly, we have to build an arsenal of new weapons—vaccines, drugs, and diagnostics.

Vaccines can be especially important in containing epidemics. But today, it typically takes up to 10 years to develop and license a new vaccine. To significantly curb deaths from a fast-moving airborne pathogen, we would have to get that down considerably—to 90 days or less.

We took an important step last month with the launch of a new public-private partnership called the Coalition for Epidemic Preparedness Innovations. The hope is that CEPI will enable the world to produce safe, effective vaccines as quickly as new threats emerge.

The really big breakthrough potential is in emerging technology platforms that leverage recent advances in genomics to dramatically reduce the time needed to develop vaccines.

This is important because we can't predict whether the next deadly disease will be one we already know, or something we've never seen before...

Of course, the preventive capacity of a vaccine won't help if a pathogen has already spread out of control. Because epidemics can quickly take root in the places least equipped to fight them, we also need to improve surveillance...

The third thing we need to do is prepare for epidemics the way the military prepares for war. This includes germ games and other preparedness exercises so we can better understand how diseases will spread, how people will respond in a panic, and how to deal with things like overloaded highways and communications systems...

Imagine if I told you that somewhere in this world, there's a weapon that exists—or that could emerge—capable of killing tens of thousands, or millions, of people, bringing economies to a standstill, and throwing nations into chaos.

You would say that we need to do everything possible to gather intelligence and develop effective countermeasures to reduce the threat.

That is the situation we face today with biological threats. We may not know if that weapon is man-made or a product of nature. But one thing we can be almost certain of. A highly lethal global pandemic will occur in our lifetimes.

When I was a kid, there was really only one existential threat the world faced. The threat of a nuclear war.

<u>By the late 1990s, most reasonable people had come to accept that climate change represented another major threat to humankind.</u>

I view the threat of deadly pandemics right up there with nuclear war and climate change. Getting ready for a global pandemic is every bit as important as nuclear deterrence and avoiding a climate catastrophe...

When the next pandemic strikes, it could be another catastrophe in the annals of the human race. Or it could be something else altogether. An extraordinary triumph of human will. A moment when we prove yet again that, together, we are capable of taking on the world's biggest challenges to create a safer, healthier, more stable world."

Now on to 2018, Gates was giving multiple warnings to multiple sources all year, way too many quotes to list here, but he keeps hounding on the need for 'germ games' like war games to create simulations in anticipation of the real deal, **which he and the WEF did in late 2019 just 6 weeks before the plannedemic began!!**

Why were unelected people like Gates & co. running germ games and not our federal government? Why not the Department of Health? Why not the CDC?

Actually, about one year before the pandemic began, Operation Crimson Contagion happened. This was a joint exercise among national, state, and local governments that was conducted from January to August 2019. This was performed coincidentally (not) just a year ahead of the worst "pandemic" in decades to happen. It was under the auspice of testing the capacity of the federal government and twelve states to be able to respond to a severe pandemic of influenza originating in… China.

The 70-page report issued after the exercise outlined the government's inept ability to respond to a pandemic. States experienced "multiple challenges" requesting resources from the federal government "due to a lack of standardized, well-understood, and properly executed resource request processes," the report stated. Basically the feds fell on their face…just like what really happened.

After Crimson Contagion, the "private sector" rolled another operation out called ***Event 201: A Global Pandemic Exercise.***

This was a simulation of a ***coronavirus*** pandemic that would go on for 18 months and go on to kill 65 million people globally.

Event 201 was an 18-month simulation crammed into a 3.5-hour presentation that you yourself can watch on YouTube as of the publishing of this book.

This was much different than Crimson Contagion though, as it was orchestrated (of course) and sponsored by (of course again) the Bill and Melinda Gates Foundation, Johns Hopkins University, and the World Economic Forum. Yes, THAT WEF!!!

The purpose of this simulation was basically to try and gauge what would happen to the world and society if a pandemic hit being as unprepared as we were. They were essentially testing the water to see if the time was right to pull the trigger on the Great Reset.

It was.

A mere 10 weeks after this simulation, the first cases of COVID-19 started showing up in Wuhan, China. That means the virus would have been released at least 3-4 weeks ahead of it becoming a threat by showing up in noticeable numbers....which means it was released about 6 weeks after Event 201!

TRILLIONS spent on "Homeland Security" since 9/11 and we weren't even prepared for a pandemic to come to our shores that was not a matter of if but when according to so many "in the know"? Give me a break!!! Why wasn't Homeland Security involved with Event 201?? We were INTENTIONALLY left wide open to what happened.

On September 29, 2019, just before the 'pandemic' started, Netflix released *"Inside Bill's Brain: Decoding Bill Gates"*.

This from the Netflix website about it: *Take a trip inside the mind of Bill Gates as the billionaire opens up about those who influenced him and the audacious goals he's still pursuing. Microsoft co-founder Bill Gates opens up about his childhood, business career and passion for improving the lives of people in the developing world.*

This is a 3-part 'investigative series' claims Netflix, but it's nothing of the sort. It's a 3-hour propaganda piece to try and make Gates look like an intelligent, caring philanthropist when he's really a diabolical, elitist eugenicist working for the Illuminati pedo-Satanists.

This was to plant the seed months before the pandemic ever appeared that Gates cares about humanity and is there to help us so you better take his advice....HA!

Next we have *"Explained: The Next Pandemic"*, released November 7, 2019...about two months before the plannedemic hit.

This was filmed months before the 'pandemic' and even predicted the next pandemic would come out of a Chinese wet market, which was in fact the official narrative according to Gates, Fauci, the CDC, the WHO, etc. ad nauseum.

Gates himself starred in this and predicted a coming pandemic...**as he's publicly predicted is coming every year since 2015.**

Finally, from Netflix, the crown jewel of predictive teevee programming of this pandemic, on January 22, 2020, they released *"Pandemic: How To Prevent an Outbreak"*, just as it was coming to light there was a novel coronavirus on the loose in China and headed our way.

This was filmed in 2018-2019.... Just months ahead of the outbreak.

On February 28, 2020, right after the 'pandemic' got going publicly, Gates released an article he penned for the prestigious New England Journal of Medicine that you should read. I'll just give a single quote from Gates here that he used to get the stampede towards the vaccines going:

"In any crisis, leaders have two equally important responsibilities: solve the immediate problem and keep it from happening again. The

Covid-19 pandemic is a case in point… Now we also face an immediate crisis. In the past week, <u>Covid-19 has started behaving a lot like the once-in-a-century pathogen we've been worried about</u>. I hope it's not that bad, but <u>we should assume it will be until we know otherwise….</u>"

Too many coincidences are piled up at this point and we're not even close to done here showing the many facets of the Great Reset.

UNITED NATIONS/AGENDA 2030

"In the event that I am reincarnated, I would like to return as a deadly virus, to contribute something to solving overpopulation."

-Prince Philip, husband of Queen Elizabeth, 1988

The people running the planet, who founded, funded and control the United Nations, are pro-population-reduction eugenicists, and the prince was doing nothing more than being candidly truthful about what the elite think of their disposable slaves on the global plantation.

Agenda 21 was a dry run for Agenda 2030, which is the real deal. They will put their foot in it to the finish line to have everything in place by 2030, and to be ready and waiting for the Antichrist to come on the scene not long after.

The United Nations' agenda 2030 has featured prominently in President Biden's agenda from the day of his inauguration.

One of the first Executive orders by Biden was one that directed the USA to rejoin the Paris Climate Accord. Adhering to the PCA will contribute greatly to the downfall of our country through carbon limits, taxes and penalties. China and India are getting off easy compared to the USA if you look into it.

Here is just the first part of this multi-page Executive Order which brought us back into the PCA:

<u>Executive Order 14008 of January 27, 2021</u>

Tackling the Climate Crisis at Home and Abroad

The United States and the world face a profound climate crisis. We have a narrow moment to pursue action at home and abroad in order to avoid the most catastrophic impacts of that crisis and to seize the opportunity that tackling climate change presents. Domestic action must go hand in hand with United States international leadership, aimed at significantly enhancing global action. Together, we must listen to science and meet the moment.

By the authority vested in me as President by the Constitution and the laws of the United States of America, it is hereby ordered as follows:

PART 1—PUTTING THE CLIMATE CRISIS AT THE CENTER OF UNITED STATES FOREIGN POLICY AND NATIONAL SECURITY

Section 101. Policy. United States international engagement to address climate change—which has become a climate crisis—is more necessary and urgent than ever. The scientific community has made clear that the scale and speed of necessary action is greater than previously believed. There is little time left to avoid setting the world on a dangerous, potentially catastrophic, climate trajectory. Responding to the climate crisis will require both significant short-term global reductions in greenhouse gas emissions and net-zero global emissions by mid-century or before.

It is the policy of my Administration that climate considerations shall be an essential element of United States foreign policy and national security....

And this EO just goes on and on and on. Biden's Executive Orders and his entire agenda is driven by the United Nation's Agenda 2030.

Now, re-read that line right above as they are telling us what is coming: ***PART 1: PUTTING THE CLIMATE CRISIS AT THE CENTER OF UNITED STATES FOREIGN POLICY AND NATIONAL SECURITY.***

You know and I know that anthropogenic climate change as the Illuminati are spinning it is a 100% provable lie. Tens of thousands of true climate experts are calling BS on this but are completely blacklisted by the controlled media because they are against the narrative, and that is the truth.

Agenda 2030 pledges to 'Leave No One Behind', they want all humans on Earth to have the same opportunities, jobs, healthcare, etc...or so they state. They aim to do this by averaging everyone out...bringing down the 1st world countries standard of living and bringing up the 3rd world countries so everyone is the 'same'. This goes hand in hand with eliminating all borders and countries, which is also part of the end goal in order to truly achieve one world government.

The **2030 Agenda for Sustainable Development** is the name of the proclamation, and a United Nations-created resolution adopted by the UN General Assembly in 2015. That gave them 15 years to accomplish their goals from 2015 to 2030.

They had planned on Hillary Clinton taking the reins the following year but we all know how that panned out.

Take four years out of that 15 years that Trump was in there and they are significantly behind, hence the Great Reset.

The Agenda 2030 goals are immediately below:

-End all poverty in all forms everywhere

-End hunger, achieve food security and improved nutrition and promote sustainable agriculture

-Ensure healthy lives and promote well-being for all at all ages

-Ensure inclusive and equitable quality education and promote lifelong learning opportunities for all

-Achieve gender equality and empower all women and girls

-Ensure availability and sustainable management of water and sanitation for all

-Ensure access to affordable, reliable, sustainable and modern energy for all

-Promote sustained, inclusive and sustainable economic growth, full and productive employment and decent work for all

-Build resilient infrastructure, promote inclusive and sustainable industrialization and foster innovation

-Reduce inequality within and among countries

-Make cities and human settlements inclusive, safe, resilient and sustainable

-Ensure sustainable consumption and production patterns

-Take urgent action to combat climate change and its impacts (acknowledging the United Nations Framework Convention on Climate Change)

-Conserve and sustainably use the oceans, seas and marine resources for sustainable development

-Protect, restore and promote sustainable use of terrestrial ecosystems, sustainably manage forests, combat desertification, and halt and reverse land degradation and halt biodiversity loss

-Promote peaceful and inclusive societies for sustainable development, provide access to justice for all and build effective, accountable and inclusive institutions at all levels

-Strengthen the means of implementation and revitalize the Global Partnership for Sustainable Development

With only ten years left to achieve the Sustainable Development Goals, world leaders at the SDG Summit in September 2019 called for a "Decade of Action" to implement Agenda 2030 by the target date of…2030. Only a couple months later the pandemic began.

In 2019 no one knew who was going to win the upcoming USA Presidential Race, and if Trump got another 4 years there was not a snowball's chance in hell of accomplishing the Illuminati's goals. Just more fuel for the fire that the election was just a sideshow and Biden was in no matter what.

This engineered storm of 'climate change' is purely to stampede humanity into the UN's waiting clutches. This physically involves using Tesla's various amazing technologies to affect the global weather and cause events that the UN is pinning on 'Climate Change.'

They even rolled out a poster-child for this scam…Greta Thunberg anyone?

Now look where we're at with 'climate change' being shoved down our throats at every mainstream media propagandized moment.

Just about all the hurricanes, fires and floods that are going on these days are not necessarily all caused by Tesla technology, but all can either be created, made worse or alleviated completely with said technology.

Not only can they affect the weather through 'geoengineering,' they can affect us personally using Tesla's technology via radio frequency (rf) waves…including being able to literally insert voices in our heads! This is a fact, unfortunately, and truly unnerving knowing they have the capability of doing this. It is important for people to be aware of things like this for what is coming so as not to be deceived.

And how about the green energy lie? Mining lithium for car batteries is one of the most toxic things you can do to the environment at every turn. And then after all that, nearly all of the energy that goes to charge the batteries come from coal, oil and gas! And they keep tearing down the dams in the name of saving the environment on top of that, and losing actual green hydropower!! Total insanity!!

Solar and wind don't make nearly the energy mankind needs, and oil products are definitely causing pollution not to mention the whole control-humanity factor.

The way out of this, and we have had the suppressed technology for years now, is liquid hydrogen.

I said it before and I'll say it again: We need to switch nearly all our energy sources to liquid hydrogen.

They say it is too dangerous but I think we can overcome that as everything else we've had to do in the past. Liquid hydrogen burns in a modified gasoline motor just like you were using liquid gasoline, but only emits water vapor and oxygen out of the exhaust! No more pollution and it's readily available because it comes from water.

A massive array of solar panels and hydroelectric could supply the pollution-free energy needed to convert water to liquid hydrogen.

The single, most-logical solution to curing "climate change," and it will never be implemented because they would lose power over it.

Great.

WORLD ECONOMIC FORUM

"The pandemic represents a rare but narrow window of opportunity to reflect, reimagine and reset our world"

-Klaus Schwab

It seems they were able to keep the WEF off everyone's radar, including mine, until it was time to roll them out of the shadows as the new and improved Bilderberg Group. Literally, the unveiling of the going-forward public face of the Illuminati, representing their direction lockstep.

What a coincidence, too. Klaus Schwab is not only a long-standing attendee of the Bilderberg Group, he was a member of the Bilderberg Steering Committee, so this guy is an elite Illuminati puppet. This is why he was put in position to create and head the WEF.

I pulled the following from an interview Euronews did with Schwab in November of 2020, nearly a year into the plannedemic:

Interviewer: I then asked Professor Schwab <u>how he intends to begin the reset</u> and where he will start. He told me there are three dimensions, three priorities:

"The first one is to make the world more resilient because <u>we definitely will have to face other surprises, black swans, as they are called, maybe different kinds of viruses.</u> Second, we have to make the world more inclusive, fairer, because we have seen that we have reached unsustainable degrees, of levels, of people who feel excluded. Finally, we have to make the world much greener. We finally have to put all our energy behind decarbonization in order to avoid a major catastrophe in the future of which we have the first signs today," Schwab added.

Let's interpret here: A 'Black Swan' is **"an <u>unpredictable or unforeseen</u> event, typically one with *extreme consequences*"**

Schwab actually put their diabolical plans into a book and it's on Amazon!

First, here is the book description from Amazon for Schwab's **'COVID-19:The Great Reset'**, published July 9, 2020:

"COVID-19: The Great Reset" is a guide for anyone who wants to understand how COVID-19 disrupted our social and economic systems, **and <u>what changes will be needed to create a more inclusive, resilient and sustainable world going forward</u>**. Klaus Schwab, founder and executive Chairman of the World Economic Forum, and Thierry Malleret, founder of the Monthly Barometer, explore what the root causes of these crisis were, and why they lead to a need for a Great Reset. Theirs is a worrying, yet hopeful analysis.

COVID-19 has created a great disruptive reset of our global social, economic, and political systems. But the power of human beings lies in being foresighted and having the ingenuity, at least to a certain extent, to take their destiny into their hands and to plan for a better future. This is the purpose of this book: to shake up and to show the deficiencies which were manifest in our global system, even before COVID broke out."

So, you mean to tell me that in under 6 months of 'pandemic', not even knowing how (allegedly) serious it was going to be until well into 2020, that Schwab was able to tie leveraging the 'pandemic' to fulfill the goals of Agenda 2030 and put it all in a book, edit it, and publish on July 9, 2020???

Not buying it. This book was written years ago to coincide with the plannedemic.

A ton of awake people have piled on in the book review section for Schwab's book, calling him and the NWO agenda to the carpet.

Here is just one review of many, the 'most helpful' ranked by readers, and this guy is AWAKE!!!:

Rated book 1 out of 5 stars ***"The Call for 'Global Governance' is Chilling"***

Reviewed in the United States on September 1, 2020

The book not only calls for 'global governance', but also for a heightened cooperation between the 'private sector' and the 'public sector'.

Private sector: banks and corporations (private interests)

Public sector: the government (public welfare)

The fact that you're trying to involve private interests in the conversation about public welfare is hilarious. Americans want a government that represents the People, not a handful of oligarchs who rig

the system to benefit themselves. America will be the greatest threat to the 'Great Reset' for this reason.

In fact, saying that 'capitalism is broken' is pretty disingenuous when you consider that banks and corporations are the ones who broke it in the first place.

Aren't we only 12 years removed from the 2008 financial crisis? And you think the people of America trust you to install 'global governance'? After our institutions have proved to be unworthy of our trust . . ?

Private sector influence in the public sector is what caused our economic woes to begin with. I seriously doubt giving banks and corporations MORE of a role in government is going to benefit us in any way. I have a radical idea: let's get money OUT of politics, not invite more of it IN.

I realize that most people don't have any economic sensibility whatsoever, but I think the WEF is underestimating the number of people who are raising eyebrows at this whole 'Great Reset' thing. Perhaps that's why radical revolutions so frequently entail locking up the educated. If you're somewhat intelligent, you see right through the lie. And so into the gulag you go! (Hopefully they have pizza in 21st century concentration camps. I need pizza.)

All in all, I was not impressed with the book. I've been paying attention to the UN's Agenda 21/2030 for awhile, but I always thought they'd pull it off a lot more smoothly than they are. As it stands right now, a lot of people are viewing this as a plot to subvert American democracy. The question is: Why isn't this big news?

-S. Lawrence

1,833 people found this helpful

I was going to go into detail about the WEF but I'll just drop the address for their website and they can tell you themselves what they have in store for us:

https://www.weforum.org

I would dare to say that pretty much everything they are talking about on the WEF website is their goal and they're not shy about telling you that they are conspiring among both corporations and governments to set the global agenda going forward.

Marvelous.

CHAPTER 4C

TURN YOU OFF

"I've got an interesting story to tell you now. There was a man named Aaron Russo, a very patriotic American who has since passed away. Mr. Russo made one of the best documentaries of all time about the New World Order agenda entitled "America: Freedom to Fascism", and I highly recommend you see it. It is available, for free, on youtube.com as of the printing of this book.

Aaron Russo was an acclaimed Hollywood producer who made the movies "Trading Places" (Eddie Murphy/Dan Akroyd) and "The Rose" (Bette Midler) among other big-name successful movies. He got into a disagreement with the IRS over some issues, which were complete BS on the part of the IRS after I learned the background facts of his story. To vent his anger he made a movie called "Mad as Hell" slamming them. Nicholas Rockefeller, son of current Rockefeller family kingpin and "head" of the American branch of the Illuminati David Rockefeller, found the movie intriguing, and after learning Russo was a big roller in Hollywood, decided he wanted to meet Aaron. The two met and became very close friends very quickly, with the friendship lasting for a few years. During this time, and approximately 11 months before 9/11 happened, Nicholas revealed to Aaron Russo the entire New World Order plan, that they were trying to implement a one world government ran by the banking industry, of which the Rockefellers are intricately part of, as you now know.

Russo, being the truly patriotic American he was, was horrified to learn the details about this, but he knew Rockefeller was telling him the truth. He ended their friendship over this information, and then went public with it after Nicholas' prophecy about 9/11 came to pass. According to Russo, Rockefeller's words on 9/11 were something along the lines of <u>"There is going to be an event soon. We're going to invade Afghanistan and our troops will be looking for terrorists in caves over there, and then we're going to invade Iraq."</u> Remember now, Russo says that Rockefeller told him this months in advance of 9/11, and it all came to pass exactly as he had said. You can hear and see Russo speak about this on a handful of clips on youtube.com.

He didn't tell Russo exactly what the event was, but it is not hard to deduce when he tells of the end result of it. He also foretells of the coming "war on terror" and how it is going to be a farce but the Mainstream Media will convince the people that it is real, and that the coming "event" is going to enable the federal government to take more and more of our liberties and freedom away. Rockefeller also revealed that they were behind the formation of the European Union, and that they were trying to form the North American Union next, by which the United States, Canada and Mexico would form a borderless community. <u>The ultimate goal, according to Rockefeller, was to implant all people of the world with RFID chips, and have all of your money and personal information contained in these chips, which they would control through the banking system that they (Illuminati) owned."</u>

–From 2013, "Rise of the New World Order 1: The Culling of Man"

In only ten years' time from the release of my first book and NO RFID chips, there are now RFID chips everywhere. Every banking or credit card has one and they won't work without them.

I remember when I got my first one of those. I promptly dug it out of the card and it worked for another 6 months using the magnetic strip-option but that soon went away and I was forced to get one for the debit card for my small handyman business. Or I wouldn't be able to do business. Ala the book of Revelation.

Your social credit score/personal RFID chip is coming ala China but there are steps in between we'll go over here. Literally, in China, if you don't conform they either fine you or flat out disable your digital money if you get out of line.

They essentially "turn you off." Now you're persona non grata.

We're not to the mark of the Beast just yet but we are surely and incrementally working our way in that direction.

Enter Bill Gates and co....

"The ID2020 Alliance" is what they are calling their little sheeple-branding project...arguably the Mark of the Beast. It's an RFID tattoo...a literal mark on your body.

Sounds inviting, doesn't it? The ID2020 Alliance. We'll all be allies together for the Green religion. Sounds like something you want to be part of...no?

Probably not, especially after I get done with them here...*cracks knuckles*

To start with, this is a United Nations-founded project.

So...the one world government predicted by the Bible is in place, the United Nations, and now they are pushing a global digital ID to track every human on the planet.

Nice. How thoughtful of them.

I don't like Wikipedia, but this is good for what we need it for…in fact REALLY good:

History: In May 2016, at the United Nations Headquarters in New York, the inaugural ID2020 summit brought together over 400 people to discuss how to provide digital identity to all, a defined Sustainable Development Goal **including to 1.5bn people living without any form of recognized identification. Experts in blockchain and other cryptographic technology joined with representatives of technical standards bodies to identify how technology and other private sector expertise could achieve the goal.**

In 2019, ID2020 started a new digital identity program in collaboration with the government of Bangladesh and vaccine alliance Gavi.

Mission: ID2020 is a public-private consortium in service of the United Nations 2030

Sustainable Development Goal of providing legal identity for ★★★*ALL*★★★ people, including the world's most vulnerable populations.

United Nations' Agenda 2030's Sustainable Development Goal 16.9: *"provide legal identity to all, including birth registration, by 2030"*

This ID system **WILL** be rolled out, in the third world to start with, but once it's established as the 'norm' it will be forced onto the first world countries.

Surprise...surprise...The Rockefeller Foundation provided the seed money to get ID2020 going through the same United Nations they founded in 1945, contributed the land for in 1946, and continue to control today.

ID2020's other contributing members include Gavi the Vaccine Alliance (Gates), Microsoft (Gates), Accenture (Microsoft/Gates business partner in other ventures) and IDEO.org (Rockefeller and Gates Foundation partner).

So this ID2020 is full-on Illuminati-Rockefeller incepted-and-directed, Epstein-Island-compromised-puppet-Gates-implemented, and it IS the one world digital ID that is coming so you better brush up on it even more than what I'm relating here. This is going to be connected to the global digital currency that will come about after the death of the fiat United States dollar and the rest of the nations' fiat currencies...part of the planned Great Reset.

This new digital ID is going to come into the first-world countries as a 'necessary evil' to track who is still standing after the Great Reset

The World Economic Forum is also involved with ID2020...of course!

There will be false-flags of all orders to help bring this in. More plannedemics. The rise of digital terrorism, people hacking the internet systems and sites and causing chaos. The WEF was just talking about this recently, even running cyberterrorism drills...keep that on your radar!!

Now this from the ID2020 website's home page:

"*__We__* need to get digital ID right. Identity is vital for political, economic, and social opportunity. But systems of identification are *__archaic, insecure, lack adequate privacy protection__*, and for over a billion people, inaccessible. Digital identity is being defined now-and *__we__* need to get it right."

Now, where it says *'we'* they don't mean you and me and them, friend. They mean themselves, the globalist NWO cabal pushing this global digital ID.

This is from the ID2020 website's "overview" page:

"ID2020 is coordinating funding for identity and channeling those funds toward high-impact projects, enabling diverse **stakeholders** - UN agencies, NGOs, governments, and enterprises - to pursue a coordinated approach that creates a pathway for efficient and responsible implementation **at scale.***"

Well, surely the ~~shareholders~~ stakeholders want their owned property to be kept track of, right? Right.

Don't farmers tag their cattle as soon as they are born? I live in the middle of cattle country and you better believe they do! Now they want to brand us like cattle…how thoughtful, they didn't want us to get lost…or more likely they want to know where you are 24/7 in case you're thinking about rebelling.

I could list quote after quote from the ID2020 website but I'll leave you just one more, from their FAQ page. You yourself should snoop through their site also and often as it's going to be changing as events unfold.

"What is a "good" digital identity?"

A "good" digital identity is one that is truly yours. With a "good" digital identity you can enjoy your rights to privacy, security, and choice.

The right to privacy is the right to permission access to your information at a granular level on an ongoing basis. Today, we consent once to give access to our digital identifiers. While it is possible in some digital spaces to revoke consent, revocation mechanisms are often esoteric and hidden behind high barriers to entry. True privacy means that you control access to individual digital identifiers, and that you can revoke (or modify) that access easily, at any time.

The right to security is all about protecting your data from unwanted access. Our certified digital identity systems must adhere to the highest security standards in existence today. And we are constantly evolving our Technical Requirements, which you can view here, in response to a changing landscape.

Last but not least, the right to choice is essential, and often overlooked in the digital world. Though you certainly have the right to choose among a few providers, and to exchange access to your information for that right, **true choices are few and far between in the digital world; to get philosophical for a moment, what freedom actually exists in a world of prescribed, circumscribed choices? A world that, in most cases, takes a certain kind of digital presence as a given?**

Achieving each of these rights depends on shifting the locus of control away from institutions and towards you.

A "good" digital identity is one that is portable, persistent, privacy-protecting, and personal.

Portability means that your information can be moved seamlessly from one hosting/storage site to another, without duplication, modification, or deletion. Persistence refers to durability; that your digital identity will stay with you for life, and that no individual or institution can duplicate, modify, or delete it. Privacy-protection refers to the safeguards in place to ensure that activities that you do not consent to are strictly forbidden. Personal means that you control your information at a granular level on an ongoing basis.

In short, a "good" digital is yours.

Basically, what I'm gathering from the above, is that the new digital ID they are proposing is mobile, is on or in you at all times, and works in conjunction with your biometrics/fingerprint/retina scanner/whatever. So some type of digital tracker/storage device...like an RFID chip... will work in conjunction with biometrics to confirm it really is you, anywhere on the globe, without an ID like a driver's license or passport you have to carry around. This will also control the digital global currency that is coming…I wonder if Slow-Kill is involved with that?

Oh wait, what's this? Microsoft recently applied for a patent for their proposed cryptocurrency (digital currency), patent # wo/2020/060606. Please take special note of the last set of numbers…. If I didn't know any better (!) I'd say the patent number looks like 06 06 06 …666…perfect.

CHAPTER 5

ENTER THE PANDEMIC

The proponents of the Great Plan have been the world's major drug suppliers, pushers, and profiteers from ancient times all the way up to today.

This is partly because mind-altering substances are typically ingested during occult ceremonies so they needed reliable access to them...so they trafficked in them and profited handsomely while denigrating the societies they ruled at the same time.

In today's times, the Illuminati-controlled CIA oversees and coordinates manufacturing illicit drugs overseas, smuggling them in and then distributing to major dealers. Society-killing drugs like cocaine, methamphetamine, and heroin, rack up billions in black market profits for the Illuminati to further use against us.

The profits of the black-market illicit drugs rival the legal drugs churned out by their multinational pharmaceutical corporations such as Pfizer, Merck, AstraZeneca and Johnson & Johnson.

The #1 best selling drug of all time, Lipitor, comes from the goliath of Big Pharma, Pfizer.

Pfizer has also had the #1 biggest government-imposed fine of all time for lying about the safety and efficacy of their drug Bextra, even encouraging off-label use for conditions deemed unsafe by the FDA approval panel. The fine was over $2 billion.

But everybody recognizes and loves Pfizer largely because of that little blue pill. And that's about all they know about Pfizer. Oh, that, and they saved the world with their breakthrough mRNA Covid vaccine.

Nobody does any research about Pfizer's checkered past before they roll the dice with some newfangled and expensive drug that was only recently approved by the FDA. If they did they might think twice about it in case they are lying about it's safety in the name of big profits.

This seemed to make them the perfect candidate to spearhead the covid vaccine drive. People were willing to look the other way with regards to their corruption. Pfizer's marketing (propaganda) team were arguably the ones handing the script to Fauci and Gates, who were the faces of the "cure" against such a deadly disease with what eventually turned out to be north of a 99.6% survival rate.

This false-flag-of-a-pandemic was never about us dealing with a random, naturally-occurring virus that the nations and governments of the world weren't prepared for.

It was about introducing an engineered bioweapon and stampeding the sheeple into a "vaccine" that they've had ready to go for a long time...for the culling of mankind.

Good night. Where to even begin with this massive false flag?

How about the fact that the seasonal flu and cold season mysteriously and conveniently disappeared in 2020-2021.

According to the CDC website on 2/25/23, there were 36 million flu cases in the 2019-20 flu season. In the 2020-21 flu season, when Covid was running rampant, there were only 9 million flu cases, a 75% reduction. Deaths from the flu for 2019-20 were estimated at 25,000, while only 5,000 for 2020-21, an 80% reduction.

According to Webmd(dot)com, 'coronavirus' variants are responsible for 20% of the annual cold season pre-pandemic. Those cases surely showed up as coronavirus infection because they are!

People WERE getting colds and the flu as usual but the way they were running the PCR tests EVERYTHING was showing positive for Covid 19.

When the President of Tanzania went public that he had results of PCR tests showing that a sample from a goat, a papaya, and a paw paw tree all tested positive for covid 19, people should have immediately started to question what was really going on…and some did.

A lot of those people who were alarmed also refused the injection when the time came, but most didn't even raise an eyebrow over long-term safety concerns, mostly because that alarm was suppressed by the controlled media.

The very man who INVENTED the PCR test, Kary Mullis, said specifically that his test was not to be used to test for viruses as it was not intended to be, nor an accurate way to test for ANY viruses or illnesses.

This is from an interview from 1993, the year he won the Nobel Prize:

"I don't think you can misuse PCR. The results, the interpretation of it if they could find this virus in you at all (talking about HIV). If you do it well you can find almost anything in anybody…it starts making you believe in the Buddhist notion that everything is contained and everything else. Because if you can amplify one single molecule up to something you can really measure, as PCR can do, then there's just very few molecules that you don't have at least one single one of them in your body so that could be thought of as a misuse of it, to claim that it's meaningful. There's very little of what they call HIV…the measurement for it is not exact at all…those (PCR tests) are all based on things that are invisible and the results are inferred. PCR is separate from that. It's just a process that is used to make a whole lot of something out of something. It doesn't tell you that you're sick…"

I'm sure Mullis would be speaking out publicly against his test being used for this depopulation operation but he conveniently DIED suddenly in August 2019 right before the plannedemic kicked off!

In fact, the CDC eventually came out—after the initial Covid vaccines were largely disbursed---and instructed testers to turn down the number of cycles because they were just then suddenly concerned about false positives…what a load of crap! The whole beginning and during the worst of the "pandemic" they were running too many cycles and people with NO symptoms were testing positive for coronavirus. Remember that?? "One of the symptoms is NO SYMPTOMS" !!!!!

And during the initial rollout of the vaccines, it seems there were no end of "issues" going on with Johnson and Johnson's and AstraZeneca's vaccines, which **_don't_** use the mRNA technology…issues that were suspiciously publicized and pushed people more and more over to seeking out the mRNA vaxxes from Moderna and Pfizer.

They had said that AstraZeneca's vaccine was causing blood clots and scared everyone over to the mRNA tech and on 4/13/21 the US federal government suspended Johnson & Johnson's vaccine because of only 6 people out of 7 million shots administered had caused the same blood clot issue. It was also announced during the hysteria that 15 million doses of JnJ's vaccine had to be destroyed due to a manufacturing error, even FURTHER pushing the population towards the mRNA vaccines.

It's not too hard to take a look into the future to see what the long-term health effects will be from taking the mRNA "vaccine". This particular vaccine is no such thing, it's actually gene therapy. Just because it comes in a syringe and is injected with a needle doesn't make it a vaccine. It is a DNA-altering technology with no published long-term side effects of turning your immune system against itself, which is exactly what it does. It just completely makes it go haywire and in which direction of ailment is anyone's guess.

This mRNA technology injection teaches your body how to make a protein-marker allegedly from the covid 19 virus. Not the virus itself, but a part of the virus called a 'spike protein' so in that way it is sort of similar to a traditional vaccine.

The big difference is that a traditional vaccine only puts a set amount of viral material for your body's immune system to target and attack.

The mRNA gene therapy programs your immune system to **create** the cytotoxic covid 19 spike protein so that your immune system can then attack it. This action would train the immune system to recognize the marker of the Covid virus and if you catch Covid 19 you can immediately fight it off...or so they said.

So. Your body's immune system is **_always_** jacked up because there is constantly Covid spike proteins being manufactured within the body that the immune system has to fight. Forever.

Long-term side effects will not be known to the public for months and years, and if it turns out the mRNA vaccine side-effects were a **_"an unforeseen and unfortunate occurrence"_** then it will be too late for billions of people.

This whole rushed-vaccine-business is why it is so critical to question how quickly they miraculously had this wonderfully safe and effective mRNA vaccine technology ready to go for not only one but two vaccines from two competing companies, Pfizer and Moderna.

Moderna is Bill Gates' pet project since 2016 when he gave Moderna $20 million to get going on the mRNA vaccine tech. This excused him from not having any kind of medical background but spoke as if he was the be-all, end-all of mRNA expertise. Gates has since made millions or more off the Moderna mRNA shots.

There is ZERO liability for Pfizer and Gates/Moderna no matter WHAT happens because it was rubber-stamped by the corrupt FDA and covered under the Vaccine Act of 1986, but you already knew that.

The reason they were able to ram this technology down our throats is that they had FDA Emergency Use Authorization/EUA to be able to skip the long-term clinical trials.

In order to get a rushed vaccine out under emergency authorization there must be no other known and *approved* treatments for the disease (as a result of clinical trials) which is why they stonewalled hydroxychloroquine, Ivermectin and other drugs which proved to work wonders against covid19.

The relentless marketing campaign to get injected came right from Big Pharma via our own government in the form of CDC and health department PSAs. They weren't commercials though (wink wink), because Big Harma can't legally advertise a product that only has emergency authorization. So how Big Pharma got around this, and this is actually even more nefarious, is they instead bankrolled your local radio, teevee and government-controlled public health departments with money for governmental 'public service announcements' which were nothing but commercials for the mRNA shots.

"SLOW KILL" BILL

Make a note and remember this future quote from Gates, Fauci, or similar in the media once they have to admit the jabs are killing people and now we've got a whole new problem to deal with:

"This was unforeseen and an unfortunate occurrence. We did the best we could with the technology we had available. It turns out Covid wasn't really that deadly after all, and the vaccine may very well kill (vastly) more people than Covid 19 the virus. You know, those conspiracy theorists were bound to get something right someday...I mean, even a broken clock is right twice a day."

Do you remember how they used the media to make sure everyone saw Bill Gates and Anthony Fauci allegedly getting their first covid vaccine shots?

Gates, Fauci and many others are well aware of the long-term effects of the initial mRNA shots so you better believe they were getting saline injections with the intent of showing you it's safe...which it wasn't...and that you can trust them...which you can't.

The public narrative put out about Gates leading up to and after the start of the Plannedemic wasn't the old-usual script of the ruthless, diabolical head of the Evil Empire itself, Microsoft. I don't think that public perception of that ever really went away, even after all the hoopla when he founded his tax-free foundation and was "giving his billions to charity".

Hopefully a lot of people saw Bill's "charity" for what it was: A way to shelter his wealth from taxes, and to help foot the bill for the Great Plan agenda of depopulation and indentured servitude for whoever is left standing.

There was a media-blitz in the months and years leading up to the 'Plannedemic', depicting Gates as a mild-mannered, sweater-wearing, caring, concerned, constantly-smiling billionaire philanthropist who is throwing billions of dollars of his own money around to make the world a safer place via vaccines.

He's no doctor, but it seemed he was an expert to most people about the covid vaccines in particular and that we were in the middle of a deadly pandemic so you better get vaccinated as soon as possible or you'll kill grandma!!

Remember when all the talking heads like Gates, Fauci, the CDC, the WHO, etc. all said FLAT OUT that if you take the covid vaccine you will not get Covid? Another of a cavalcade of proven lies. I've seen video compilations on Facebook of them saying exactly this and other outright falsities…fake news!!!

Gates in particular needs to account for what he's done as the unofficial private-sector rep against the pandemic, but he's been rotten long before that.

Gates was born and raised an elitist eugenicist because that's what his family was about.

According to a quote from Slow Kill Bill himself, his lawyer-dad was head of the murder-for-profit Planned Parenthood for a while, and his moral compass was the guide for Bill's upbringing.

"When I was growing up, my parents were always involved in various volunteer things. My dad was head of Planned Parenthood, and it was very controversial to be involved with that."
–Bill Gates from 'NOW with Bill Moyers'. 5/9/03

Gates pursues his father-instilled eugenicist ambitions by bankrolling the World Health Organization, an arm of the UN, and the CDC, an arm of Big Pharma. By working with these organizations and others he "donates" billions to in order to facilitate "vaccine development and technology in general that will help bring the third world up out of poverty."

Gates and his puppetmaster-Illuminati have no intention of bringing the third world standard of living up to the first world standard. They are seeking to do the EXACT OPPOSITE! The citizens of the USA, Europe and other first world nations are soon to know what it feels like to starve, even to death.

"First, we've got population. The world today has 6.8 billion people. That's headed up to about nine billion. Now, if we do a really great job on new vaccines, health care, reproductive health services, we could lower that by, perhaps, 10 or 15 percent ..."
–Bill Gates, 2010 'TED talk'

When Gates says "reproductive health services" he means that his people are actively sterilizing and euthanizing Africans and Asians via vaccines, birth control and abortions!

Here is a portion of a transcript of that interview between Bill Moyers and Bill Gates in 2003:

GATES: *Certainly, I'll never be able to put myself in the situation that people growing up in the less developed countries are in. I've gotten a bit of a sense of it by being out there and meeting people and talking with them. And one of the gentlemen I met with AIDS talked about how he'd been kicked out of where he'd lived and how he felt awful he'd given it to his wife and their struggle to make sure their child didn't have it, and the whole stigma thing, which, you know, that's hard to appreciate. In this country when you get sick people generally reach out, you know, that's the time to help other people and yet some of these diseases it's quite the opposite.*

So, what I was thinking about was where my resources that I'm the steward of be able to make an impact, I thought "okay, what's the greatest inequity left?" And to me, and the more I learned about health and the unbelievable inequity, it kind of stunned me, it shocked me, every step of the way.

MOYERS: *You could have chosen any field, any subject, any issue and poured billions into it and been celebrated. How did you come to this one? To global health?*

GATES: *The two areas that are changing in this amazing way are information technology and medical technology. Those are the things that the world will be very different 20 years from now than it is today.*

I'm so excited about those advances. And they actually feed off of each other. The medical world uses the information tools to do their work. And so when you have those advances you think will they be available to everyone. Will they not just be for the rich world or even just the rich people and the rich world? Will they be for the world at large?

The one issue that really grabbed me as urgent were issues related to population... reproductive health.

And maybe the most interesting thing I learned is this thing that's still surprising when I tell other people which is that, as you improve health in a society, population growth goes down.

You know I thought it was...before I learned about it, I thought it was paradoxical. Well if you improve health, aren't you just dooming people to deal with such a lack of resources where they won't be educated or they won't have enough food? You know, sort of a Malthusian view of what would take place.

And the fact that health leads parents to decide, "okay, we don't need to have as many children because the chance of having the less children being able to survive to be adults and take care of us, means we don't have to have 7 or 8 children." Now that was amazing.

MOYERS: *But did you come to reproductive issues as an intellectual, philosophical pursuit? Or was there something that happened? Did come up on... was there a revelation?*

GATES: *When I was growing up, my parents were always involved in various volunteer things. My dad was head of Planned Parenthood. And it was very controversial to be involved with that. And so it's fascinating. At the dinner table my parents are very good at sharing the things that they were doing. And almost treating us like adults, talking about that.*

Do you understand what Gates was saying when he said when you improve health the population goes down? If you're loading up people with slow-kill vaccines of course it does, let alone an "unforeen" mass kill event. This was just doublespeak to cover up his intentions of using vaccines to not only decrease the global population but to CULL it.

Fast forward 20 years from that interview and here we are.

It should be noted that Bill Sr., Bill Jr. And Melinda are all card-carrying, pro-New World Order Progressives. They are all pro-abortion, pro-open borders, pro-globalist, etc. You know...the NWO-crowd.

In the 2016 Wikileaks dump it was even revealed that Hillary Clinton had considered Bill Gates as her VP pick!!

Melinda Gates, speaking at the 2019 G7, pushed for digital currency in order to help empower women. Melinda is a known Bilderberg attendee, as is Bill.

Gates was recently busted associating with notorious pedophile and child-trafficker Jeffrey Epstein. Gates' name is in many of the flight manifests on the 'Lolita Express' to Epstein's Pedo-Island in the Caribbean.

Sounds like a real wholesome guy, right? Someone you would trust your life to, right? WRONG!

How did this punk Bill Gates get the money and power needed to realize his father's ambitions? He schemed, bullied and pirated his way to the top just like a punk does ala John D. Rockefeller.

Bill Gates Jr. was positioned with $50,000 from somewhere to purchase the program that would become MS-DOS...Gates didn't invent anything!! He then got his foot in the door to license this product to IBM in a hugely shady deal if you investigate it...thanks, Mom!!

I'm starting to think Gates was picked long ago for the role he played in the pandemic the way his life went.

It was revealed in his Microsoft co-founder Paul Allen's memoir, "Idea Man", that Allen stated Gates was a ruthless schemer who demeaned his employees and conspired to rip him off personally of his percentage of Microsoft ownership!!

He stated that Gates was after every bit of the company he could get when it came time to issue stock and Allen felt bullied, getting less of a share than he felt he deserved. Allen also stated he overheard Gates and Steve Ballmer conspiring against him to lessen his stake in the company even more!! Gates is truly a punk that thinks little of humanity like he does his employees. This is documented in co-founder Allen's book!

Gates brutish approach to business and competition that led Microsoft to the top peaked in February of 2000 when he was forced to step down as CEO of Microsoft as part of a deal with US government prosecutors over anti-trust legislation against Microsoft.

Gates bowed out of Microsoft with billions upon billions of dollars' worth of stock.

Now, Gates is way up the financial ladder but remember, he's no Rockefeller. Gates' billions **PALE IN COMPARISON TO THE TRILLIONS CONTROLLED BY THE PROPONENTS OF THE GREAT PLAN.**

Gates is a PIKER. A PUPPET. Why do you think he was caught photographed with Jeffrey Epstein? To compromise him to the NWO puppet masters.

You've never seen and will never see a Rothschild or Rockefeller with Epstein or in any of his 'Lolita Express' jet airplane flight manifests. But they got Gates' hands dirty with Epstein and arguably even before that.

The Satanic Rothschild/Rockefeller/Royal Family are the pinnacle of the global Satanic network. Notice how Prince Andrew got tangled up with Epstein and walked away scot-free even with victim eyewitness testimony against him IN PUBLIC...he was never meant to be compromised like Gates or others as he was born into the BIG CLUB.

So Gates, not wanting to keep all his financial-power eggs in one basket, or his fingers in one piece of the NWO-pie as it were, Gates started getting involved in all manners of NWO-related mechanisms to destroy the USA after establishing his tax-free foundation.

Let's start with the organized dumbing down of America called 'Common Core.' Yes, Gates is primarily responsible for Common Core!!! A dumbed-down America would be much easier to compromise and then collapse, making them dependent on a world government to save them from themselves.

Starting with $200 million in 2008, Gates bankrolled the program and also the political strings that needed to be pulled in order to institute Common Core nationwide…which they did.

Once Obama got sworn in at the start of 2009, the then-President Obama swiftly worked to implement Gates' Common Core nationwide. Just a couple of good ol' modern day progressives looking out for the USA…ugh.

10+ years, $400+ million of Gates Foundation money, hundreds of billions of taxpayer-education funds, and a ruined generation later, Gates finally admitted Common Core was a failure in 2017.

Wow. See how much *evil* influence this guy has already had over us and our nation? He never intended to make our kids smarter at all, quite the opposite!!! He is a full-on NWO-puppet boy.

After Gates started his foundation and had access to tax-free money, he started to diversify his holdings….

In 2010 he threw out some pocket change to the tune of $23 million and bought 500,000 shares of Monsanto.

He stated the following on GMOs in a 2016 Wall Street Journal interview:

"What are called GMOs are done by changing the genes of the plant, and it's done in a way where there's a very thorough safety procedure, and it's pretty incredible because it reduces the amount of pesticide you need, raises productivity (and) can help with malnutrition by getting vitamin fortification. And so I think, for Africa, this is going to make a huge difference, particularly as they face _climate change_ …"

He sure seems to slam home how safe everything he is involved in is. And you better believe he's one of the international doomsayers about man-made "Climate Change".

The fact is that most GMO crops are intended to be bathed in the toxic weedkiller Roundup, which contains cancer-causing Glyphosate, the active ingredient in Monsanto's 'Roundup' weed killer.

The crops are genetically altered to be able to withstand the Roundup, but the weed killer kills everything else around it, including the people, and then goes on to contaminate the soil, water, air and everything else. Search to see that Roundup is factually present in nearly all breakfast cereals and in disturbing amounts. I'll never eat Frosted Flakes again!!

I've looked extensively into Roundup/glyphosate and it is just toxic, let alone the other even WORSE chemicals that are put in it that are labeled 'inert ingredients' making them immune from listing on the label!!!

I saw that Gates had recently partnered with global AG magnate Cargill to start introducing GMO soy into Africa. So the people there are already starving and toxified from Gates' vaccines for malaria, etc. so now Gates wants to give them Frankenfood that that have to bathe in toxic chemicals to make work and poison their land and people. Perfect.

In 2016 Bayer bought Monsanto, kept their products/name brands, and dropped the Monsanto name. The toxic products are still there, just under the wholesome **Bayer** banner.

This is the same Bayer that, among other things, **kept HIV-infected medicines on the market in third world countries after pulling them in the USA after it was discovered they were contaminated with HIV**....they literally murdered thousands of people with their tainted medicine for hemophiliacs, most of them children.

Moving on to the next NWO-themed action Gates has inserted himself in....

At the end of 2018, it was publicly announced that Bill Gates would be teaming up with Harvard scientists...meaning he was bankrolling them and they would be answering to him...to do experiments in injecting solid particles into the atmosphere to block the Sun in the hopes of mitigating 'climate change'. Hey Gates! You might want to talk to the military black ops, they have been spraying us like bugs for YEARS and are PROS at blocking out the Sun on any given day via chemtrails.

To mitigate cow farts (!), it was also recently announced that Gates was teaming up with Tyson Foods and others to start making artificial meat to combat climate change by getting rid of the global-warming methane gas emanating from both ends of millions of cows. This meat would take cultured meat cells and regrow the meat in laboratories.

Mmmmmm...tasty labmeat....soylent green can't be far behind at this point.

So...on to the Big Kahuna that Gates has taken upon himself: Vaccines

To start with, the Gates Foundation donations to the World Health Organization/WHO are second only to the United States contributions. This is the group who gets to decide when a disease 'officially' turns into a global 'pandemic.' They are also the front that Gates uses to inject (!) his influence into third world countries and ultimately the entire planet.

The WHO is an arm of the United Nations, and you know who founded and runs the UN.

Baal Gates has taken Harmageddon to dizzying new heights since marshalling himself up as Captain Jabbin' and carpet bombing the third world with vaccines. Under the authority of the UN/WHO of course.

Bill Gates, a white, elitist-eugenicist leftist, is bankrolling the eradication of the third world brown and black people. I'm surprised he's not a GOD in the white supremacist/KKK community!

Gates funded GlaxoSmithKline's experimental malaria vaccine that killed 151 African infants and caused paralysis, seizures, and convulsions to 1,048 of the 5,049 children administered the vaccine...**that's a 20% serious side effect rate right out of the gate!!**

In India, Gates experimental polio vaccine, which upped the standard schedule of 5 to **50** polio vaccine doses/injections PER CHILD, paralyzed 480,000 Indian children between 2000 and 2017.

In 2017 the WHO reluctantly admitted that the global polio explosion was predominately vaccine strain, **meaning it came from Gates' vaccines!!!**

WHERE IS THE MAINSTREAM MEDIA ON THIS AND OTHER ATROCITIES!!!! **It is estimated that in 2018, ¾ of all global polio cases were from Gates' vaccines.**

In 2014, Gates funded the experimental HPV vaccine on 23,000 unwitting and unwilling girls in India with a handful dying and 1,200 suffering side effects including autoimmune and fertility disorders. Indian government investigators charged that Gates-funded researchers committed atrocious ethical violations during the course of the trials including bullying parents, forging consent forms, and refusing medical care to the injured girls!!

Gates & co. supplied the WHO with billions and in turn they chemically sterilized millions of Kenyan women with a tetanus sterility formula vaccine!! You can't make this stuff up!!

Gates also funded Johns Hopkins University experiments that intentionally infected hundreds of Guatemalans with sexually transmitted diseases for drug and vaccine testing.

If Gates was running around the United States using us as guinea pigs like he has done in the third world he'd be taking a dirt nap and pushing up daisies by now but instead the Deep State PROTECTS HIM by using the WHO/CDC/NIH/etc. as fronts to shield his murderous intentions and actions in the third world.

Ever hear of the Tuskegee Experiment? Look into **THAT** to see just what the people in charge of your health here in the USA can pull on you!! Especially if you're BLACK!!

Gates has hijacked the WHO agenda away from those programs that would most benefit the Third World peoples in the fight against disease. You know, things like clean water, hygiene, good nutrition, antibiotics, healthy economy, etc.

Apparently, Gates thinks good health only comes from a syringe or he'd be funding everything I just listed equally or more so as he does vaccines but no, it's all depop-shots from Gates.

"One of the questions I get asked the most these days is when the world will be able to go back to the way things were in December (2019) before the coronavirus pandemic. My answer is always the same: when we have an almost perfect drug to treat COVID-19, or when almost every person on the planet has been vaccinated against coronavirus.

The former is unlikely to happen anytime soon. We'd need a miracle treatment that was at least 95 percent effective to stop the outbreak. Most of the drug candidates right now are nowhere near that powerful. They could save a lot of lives, but they aren't enough to get us back to normal.

Which leaves us with a vaccine.

Humankind has never had a more urgent task than creating broad immunity for coronavirus. Realistically, if we're going to return to normal, we need to develop a safe, effective vaccine. We need to make billions of doses, we need to get them out to every part of the world, and we need all of this to happen as quickly as possible.

That sounds daunting, because it is. Our foundation is the biggest funder of vaccines in the world, and this effort dwarfs anything we've ever worked on before. It's going to require a global cooperative effort like the world has never seen. But I know it'll get done. There's simply no alternative."

–Bill Gates, April 30, 2020 on his blog

Gates has also said he wants death panels installed via the health system to determine if your life is worth saving when you are older and a 'burden' to society.

"...spending a million dollars on that last three months of life for that patient or laying off ten teachers. But that's called the death panel and you're not supposed to have that discussion..."
–Bill Gates, speaking at the 2010 Aspen Ideas Festival, Aspen, Colorado.

Gates miraculously had the foresight to invest in BioNTech (partner of Pfizer's mRNA covid vaccine) just months before the plannedemic and made hundreds of millions of dollars when BioNTech's stock skyrocketed upon the release of the "Pfizer" vaccine.

On April 12, 2020, Bill Gates was interviewed on the "BBC Morning" show...

Interviewer Charlie/BBC: *As you'll be aware, a lot of people in the UK are asking, what is it, a very simple and straightforward question, which is "When will there be a vaccine?" How do you see that?*

Bill Gates: Well, that's a perfect question, because we want to get back to the life we had before coronavirus. People are seeing the economic destruction, the psychological stress...this is such an unprecedented... uhh...a very tough thing to deal with. People like myself and Tony Fauci are saying 18 months. If everything went perfectly we could do slightly better than that...but there will be a trade-off...*we'll have less safety testing than we typically would have so governments will have to decide, you know, do they indemnify the companies and really say "let's go out with this"...uhh...when we just don't have the time to do what* *we normally do*. So 18 months is about what we'd expect, we're doing everything we can...you know...we'll write checks to those factories faster than governments can...then they'll come along...it shouldn't be limited...it should be all the best constructs...full speed ahead.... science limited.

Interviewer Charlie/BBC: *Sounds like from what you're saying is it may be that there needs to be some compromise in some of the safety measures that would normally be expected to create a vaccine because time is so crucial.*

Bill Gates: Well, of course...if you want to wait and see if a side effect shows up two years later...uhh...that takes two years. So..uhh... whenever you're acting quickly, like during the HIV crisis, they created a...a...quick way of getting drug approval. There is a trade-off there... uhh...in that case it worked super, super well...and here we have... will...I think be able to get some safety indications...but...this is a "public good"...and...so you know...***those tradeoffs***...the government is working on a proper basis and will be involved in the decision to say..."Hey, the regulator says go ahead ***even though you haven't taken the normal time period***."

Interviewer Charlie/BBC: *World leaders now are listening in a way they didn't out of necessity, bearing in mind, and I know you referenced it before, in 2015 you gave those TED talks, and if people go back and listen to it now.. uh..it was extraordinarily close to what is happening now. You were talking about the real risk of a pandemic across the world. Did you feel like you were listened to then?*

Bill Gates: No. The investments that could've been done so that diagnostics would have been essentially immediately available...drugs in less than half the time...the vaccine in less than half the time...uh... most of those investments were not made. Now, SEPI is the exception to that but that's about 5% of what could have been done...uhh...now we're scrambling and it's taking us much longer for us to get these pieces together even though scientists are doing heroic work. So, you know, unlike the defense budget that prepares us for war...where we simulate the problem to make sure we're good at it...this risk, which I viewed as even greater than the risk of war...there was very, very little preparation...very few of these "germ games" where you try out...say... ok how do you build up the ICU capacity...you know...can you make that to leaders...how do you prioritize diagnostics... that we're just figuring out as we go.

Interviewer Charlie/BBC: *Was that, you think, partly a financial decision? It wasn't deemed to be worth investing that money in something maybe other people didn't see as clearly as you?*

Bill Gates: Well, it's got to be governments because...uhh...there's no private sector incentive...uhh...for something that's uncertain like this and even when it happens...uhh...you know you have to charge mostly a break-even price for things that are helping out with a global crisis like this so..."

Bill Gates agrees that there WILL be a trade-off for rushing the jabs. After all, if you want to wait two years to see if there are any real long-term side effects...that takes two years and people wanted to get back to normal NOW.

When the torches are lit and the pitchforks and nooses come out, Gates will be able to point to interviews just like this one in particular and say "I tried to warn you. Look, it's the government's fault, it was THEIR decision to allow this, not mine."

And when the first world nations' people are dropping like flies they will get no sympathy from the rest of the citizens of the world, saying we got everything we deserved for putting ourselves first to be vaccinated, first for boosters...and first for 'long term' side effects.

CHAPTER 5B

DR. DEATH 2020

Now let's get to Fauci, the public-sector rep to prop up the 'deadly' pandemic narrative and subsequent mandatory medical procedures for many millions of unlucky, naive Americans.

Anthony Fauci was born in Brooklyn in 1940, the son of a pharmacist. He was raised in a strict Roman Catholic household, first Communion at 7 and confirmed at 12 years of age.

He was schooled by Jesuits at Regis High School in New York City, and went to College of the Holy Cross, Founded in 1843 by the Society of Jesus (Jesuits) in Worcester, Massachusetts, and should be regarded as a Jesuit agent on your NWO scorecard.

Well, the love of Jesus Christ allegedly wasn't spiritually fulfilling enough for Fauci after he left school and ultimately came to be what is called a 'humanist'...by his own admission.

"Broadly and generically, I'm not a regular church attender. I have evolved into less a Roman Catholic religion person [to] someone who tries to keep a degree of spirituality about them. I look upon myself as a humanist. I have faith in the goodness of mankind."

-Anthony Fauci (this from an interview with 'the-scientist.com' in May 2003)

Goodness of mankind?? I've been keeping track of this monster from the start of the Plannedemic.

This is the same Dr. Fauci who tortured dogs to death in his lab, setting Sand Flies upon their faces by the hundreds to eat them alive while their bodies were tied down. Then, when he tired of hearing their screams, he severed their vocal cords! People who torture animals to death are soulless creatures capable of incredible evil and he was certainly the man for the depop job.

I'm sure shuttering all the churches and the arrests of clergymen and parishioners put a smile on Fauci's face. I've researched Fauci and found not one reference to his belief in, or worship of, Jesus. Plenty of talk about being educated by Jesuits though...**and how they profoundly influenced him.**

I wonder if Fauci has taken the Jesuits' Extreme Oath of Induction? Someone should ask him!!

Humanists are typically of the mantra 'if it feels good do it' or more accurately 'do what thou wilt shall be the whole of the law' ala Aleister Crowley.

They are pro-LGBTQ lifestyle, pro-abortion, pro-transhumanism, pro-genetically modifying anything possible, along those lines. Basically, science and everything it can do for humanity is your god, just as the NWO teaches. After all, science, and everything it can do is going to bring their god back to life.

Here's something with too much detail to get into here and is for you to follow up on: A former colleague of Dr. Fauci who had a falling out with him, Dr. Judy Mikovits, has gone public and on record in interviews stating that it is her position that Dr. Fauci quashed evidence she had about the HIV epidemic years ago that resulted in MILLIONS OF DEATHS WORLDWIDE. If what she was saying wasn't true, she could be sued but then all the facts would come out in court and Fauci can't have that, so he slanders and stonewalls her.

Mikovits' character has since been assassinated by the mainstream media and others but if you listen to everything that happened without blinders you will see that she is telling the TRUTH and has been vilified for it because it paints Fauci in an unfavorable light.

The mainstream media built Fauci up to be a hero, someone we could trust to tell us the new vaccines were indeed safe and effective.

The press called him 'America's Doctor' and pushed him up the pop-culture ranks by showcasing all the mugs, bobbleheads, etc. that were being churned out (in China) that paid homage to this new American hero.....*gag*

He was alleged by many to be a tyrant in his department at the NIH, bullying underlings, firing them if they had research he wanted to claim for his own. Fauci owns many vaccine-related patents, etc. If this guy was pro-humanity why is he patenting anything let alone life-saving vaccines?

So not only is Baal Gates a card-carrying, socialist, globalist leftist, it appears that ol' Tony is too.

In emails released by Wikileaks in 2016, there is an email from Anthony Fauci to Cheryl Mills, a top Clinton aide at the time, on the date Hillary Clinton testified about Bengazi, January 23, 2013.

Now we all know from looking into it that Hillary is GUILTY of TREASON and directly responsible for the deaths of four United States citizens among other alleged actions that came out of Benghazi.

Fauci had watched the hearing earlier in the day and sent the following email intending his well-wishes to be passed on to Killary:

Cheryl:

Anyone who had any doubts about the Secretary's stamina and capability following her illness had those doubts washed away by today's performance before the Senate and the House. She faced extremely difficult circumstances at the Hearings and still she hit it right out of the park. Please tell her that we all love her and are very proud to know her.

Warm regards,
Tony

Fauci has been head of the NIH's National Institute of Allergy and Infectious Diseases since 1984....and he's the highest paid federal employee to boot! Him! Fauci is! Unreal.

I cannot find any evidence or documentation anywhere that shows that Fauci has petitioned the NIH, the WHO, the Congress or any of the handful of Presidents that he served under that we needed to establish some kind of 'pandemic panel' or 'pandemic task force' or anything of the sort. Don't you think as the number 1 guy on the topic that he should have been clamoring for action....**KNOWING THAT A PANDEMIC WAS NOT A MATTER OF IF BUT WHEN?????? AT LEAST ACCORDING TO FAUCI AND SLOW KILL!!**

Instead of telling us all to prepare against a coming pandemic, he was busy creating patents for vaccines that could be sold in a pandemic to make him and others insane money, namely Gates & co.

We've spent TRILLIONS on 'national defense' but not a damn DIME on preparing for a pandemic? They left us wide open for this false flag to destroy the United States…INTENTIONALLY!

Thanks to the FOIA requests/responses, whistleblower leaks, and general human incompetence, virtually everything about the planning and execution of the false-flag plannedemic is now public knowledge if you go looking.

Fauci was caught red-handed when the NIH outed his role in the funding of the Wuhan lab weaponizing viruses to start with.

Fauci's email leak of over 3,200 emails contained messages from Fauci which said that masks don't work and Hydroxychloroquine indeed does work quite well against covid among other things!

According to the emails, the 'rona was a biological weapon made in China at the Wuhan lab with American funding, provided by Fauci. Fauci also encouraged his friends to stock up on HCQ to prevent serious illness while at the same time publicly demanding it not be prescribed to patients in order to qualify the new experimental covid vaccines for EUA! The only way to get an Emergency Use Authorization from the FDA is to have no other treatments available for a certain illness!!!!

THE VIRUS

On March 1, 2023, FBI Chief Christopher Wray stated that the covid pandemic most likely originated from a lab leak in Wuhan. This is confirmation by the head of the FBI that it was indeed a bioweapon.

This is something I've maintained since March of 2020, page 4, in my first update report about the status of the plannedemic 3 years prior!!

About time the feds said something! They've been awfully quiet since it was revealed that Ecohealth Alliance, a US NGO and funded by the NIH/National Institute of Health/Fauci, was funding bat coronavirus research in Wuhan, China.

It was not a leak from this lab, though, this is a red herring to be sure. It was an occult black op: The intentional release of a man-made virus to initiate a global false flag "deadly pandemic", with the end game being to bring on the Great Reset.

The barely-a-bioweapon (99.6% or better survival rate) was released in Wuhan, China, knowing that with the power of the media and corrupt leaders it could be used to cripple the global economy and the Western nations in particular.

It was not even as dangerous as the flu, but the controlled media and government built up a giant charade that it was a deadly, natural-occurring virus from bats, bred in a disgusting, condemnable Chinese wet market where you can purchase virtually any animal in existence for food or traditional medicine…including bats!

The Illuminati puppets painted such a dreadful, ominous, incoming death wave that if we didn't immediately go on the offensive, it would be the end of mankind.

That's where the faulty PCR test, inflated statistics, media blitz, forced masking, space-distancing, shutdowns, and general violation of humanities' civil rights came in. And, oh yeah, 4 experimental vaccines to try and salvage some of humanity. Only the weapon wasn't the virus, it was the "cure," something that was schemed years ago.

Enter Operation Warp Speed from the Trump administration on May 15, 2020.

What does that mean, "warp speed", anyways…? Warp speed, according to definition, is faster than the speed of light, much faster.

This OWS will be partially blamed for rushing and pushing the 'experimental' vaccines out and unintentionally harming the global population. You better believe Trump will be at least partially blamed for what's coming!

I would be willing to bet that the vast majority of asleep people who came across my first book and read it, and understood it, before all this happened didn't get the shot.

However…

Virtually all my family and friends, save my inner circle, took the bait and got injected with mystery liquid…containing any number of biohazardous materials it seems.

At the beginning of the pandemic in April 2020, a HIGHLY CREDIBLE person came forth stating that Covid-19 was a man-made virus and did NOT come out of a 'wet market in Wuhan'.

Luc Montagnier (RIP), the French virologist and **Nobel Prize winner** for his work on HIV, said the SARS-CoV-2 virus (COVID-19) was created in a laboratory by inserting genes from HIV, the AIDS virus, into a coronavirus!!!

"We have concluded that this virus was created," said the French scientist, during an interview with the French channel CNews.

In 2008 Montagnier won the Nobel Prize in Medicine for his part in research that led to the discovery of HIV, so this guy isn't some dummy!

"There has been a manipulation of the virus: at least part of it, not all of it. There is one model, which is the classic virus, which comes mainly from bats, but to which HIV sequences have been added, in any case, it's not natural. It's the work of professionals, of molecular biologists. Very meticulous work. For what purpose? I don't know. One hypothesis is that they wanted to create an AIDS vaccine"

Montagnier went on to cite a study by a group of researchers at the Indian Institute of Technology in New Delhi, which found "an uncanny resemblance" and "little chance of coincidence" in the amino acid sequences of a SARS-CoV-2 and HIV-1 protein.

Montagnier also predicted COVID-19 would be going away soon, its artificial origin would be weakening it.

"One can do anything with nature, but if you make an artificial construction, it is unlikely to survive. Nature loves harmonious things; what is alien, like a virus coming from another virus, for example, is not well tolerated. So what we're seeing is that in the western United States, in Seattle, the sequences are destroyed, virtually non-existent. So, if the pathogenic power of the coronavirus is linked to the insertion of these sequences, we can think that it's going to disappear."

I agreed at the time and still do today. The first version of covid 19 was soon going to disappear, and the first version of it certainly did. It's gone. Non-existant today according to all.

And then the variants began…

These were simply different engineered versions of the original covid-19 bioweapon. Every time there was a variant, it had to be released. No one knew for certain it would mutate but Gates, Fauci, the WHO, the corrupt CDC and all the rest of the 'experts' all stating waves of pandemic were coming in order to get more shots, boosters, into the sheep.

Fauci went public numerous times early and mid-2020 to state that COVID-19 is a NATURALLY OCCURRING VIRUS and at that point everyone paying attention knew that was a flat-out lie!

Nobel Prize-winner Montagnier's testimony was completely whitewashed by the mainstream media, but I've checked recently and his testimony from April 2020 remains on the web.

He unfortunately died (!) on February 8th, 2022, not long after going public with claims that anyone who is taking the mRNA shots is essentially giving themselves AIDS.

RIP Mr. Montagnier. Thank you for your truth and service.

CHAPTER 5D

PAPERS...PLEASE.

"Americans should pause and reflect on the lies they are being sold. Masks are just a form of psychological manipulation. Many reputable physicians and scientists have said they are worthless and potentially harmful. Lockdowns are meant to condition people to obey without question. A nation of people who just do what they are told by the 'experts' is a nation ripe for a descent into total tyranny."

–Dr. Ron Paul, patriot and former United States Congressman for over 20 years

By now, you know as well as I do that Covid-19 was no deadlier than any average strain of flu and since society has always just powered through any average flu pandemic in the past, that is what we **SHOULD** have done.

In any flu season, employees would just have to take their turn getting sick like we always have. If enough employees got sick that company would shut down for a couple of weeks or whatever **BY THEIR OWN MANAGEMENTAL DECISION** and then get back to work at their own discretion. No government mandates, shutting down and laying people off, stimulus checks, any of it.

But this wasn't any pandemic, it was and still is a plannedemic.

And people were so traumatized and scared of dying from covid that they were tattling/turning each other in for violating rules that violated our Constitutional rights. See how easy that was? People wonder how a government can happen like that, something like Nazi Germany, but you've already witnessed it with your own two eyes.

Towards the alleged end of the pandemic, the political left is now fully onboard with the NWO agenda and has virtually morphed into the party of the New World Order. You can expect many more voting shenanigans going forward to make sure the right people get into the right positions such as Joe Biden.

Welcome to the USSA.

The mandatory mask wearing/social distancing for a virus no deadlier than the flu was to convince the world to get used to being under the bureaucratic jackboot and put police in charge of enforcing unjust, unfair and oppressive actions which further divides the people between public and government.

If masks really worked why did they release all the inmates by the thousands "for their own safety".

Why did Mom and Pop stores have to stay closed if the masks work?

Why were you able to go to Walmart or Target but not Granny's Antique Store in your hometown?

Most people had no clue that the masks don't protect you from getting COVID-19. If that were the case scientists working on virus research wouldn't be in a completely enclosed HAZMAT suit!!

Even an N95-rated mask is basically a sneeze guard. Nothing short of a full-face respirator with filter cartridges...literally a gas mask... would protect you from a virus.

On one hand you've got a surveillance–police state rising, on the other hand as in my state of Washington, police hands are tied and you can't even pursue a car involved in a crime because it "endangers the citizens"!!!

The criminals know this now and the crime rate is exploding in Seattle. I ran that city all over as a kid but now have absolutely no reason whatsoever to set foot there ever again.

Drugs have also been decriminalized or even cops told not to do anything about it in my state and also Oregon because black and brown people are more likely to be involved with drugs than white people??? You're not doing them any favors by condoning highly self-destructive behavior!

What is the result of literally legislating into reality this bizzarro-world?

Increased crime across all categories....DUH!!

We essentially had 'soft' martial law in the United States before and during the rollout of the experimental vaccines with mandatory vaccinations under governmental and globalist corporate requirements for terms of employment and access to certain public places like concerts and restaurants and other 'fun' things to do.

They made it as miserable as possible so people would want to take the vaccines to get life back to normal.

All the state workers, health professionals, firemen, police, etc. were all required to be vaccinated in Washington state at that time.

They injected all the essential workers and military in Washington state with an experimental vaccine, that you now know was not experimental but a proven biohazard.

In my state, you needed to provide proof you had taken the jab to live 'normally', but were now a guinea pig for long-term side effects under fascist duress.

We're there. Or at least we were. But it will surely be back, mark my words.

Welcome to the Fourth Reich...papers...*please.*

CHAPTER 5E

COERCION OF CONFORMITY

"The most brilliant propagandist technique will yield no success unless one fundamental principle is borne in mind constantly: It must confine itself to a few points and repeat them over and over."

-Adolf Hitler's Minister of Propaganda, Dr. Joseph Goebbels

Let's see...what would be a good example of the words heard most out of the mouths of those encouraging us all to get vaxxed?

"Safe and effective" ring a bell?

How about "Climate Change" ...oops...wrong psyop.

How about "Free donuts with proof of vaccination" ...LMAO!

Literally. For like a year after they started offering the clotshots you could get a free donut every day at the local Krispy Kreme. Just flash your vaxcard and you're good to go. See you tomorrow, Joe Average American, because nothing says healthy living like experimental gene-therapy with a deep-fried donut on the side.

And then we had the gambling element come into play...you couldn't make this stuff up on a dare! I thought this was about public health, not promoting the Seven Deadly Sins all at once!

Again. Literally. You could enter online in Washington state to win various amounts of lottery money for the vaccinated only! I don't remember paying my taxes to give away promoting depopulation!!

And then they had one for the vaccinated servicemen and women of the local armed forces! That hit me pretty hard knowing the most patriotic Americans of all were being pied-pipered into taking the shots.

Then we had bribing by the feds of hospitals/doctors/nurse for positive covid tests, hospitalizations, ventilators, deaths attributed to covid, etc.

They got a whole menu of money that they could get by making sure the above actions not only were documented but actively pursued to bring in federal money they spread all over the map to ensure big covid casualty numbers...to help convince everyone to take the vaccine.

They pushed hard. And we haven't even gotten to the media's side of pushing the narrative of a highly-deadly pandemic with an experimental vaccine as the only way out, but I digress.

Now that the mask-mandates are largely gone, there are people who will still wear them FOREVER because they have truly been terrorized by this false flag operation.

These were the people first in line for the initial jabs and the boosters and they're just miserable people because they're scared to death of dying from covid and now they've been injected full of poison...and they'll still get covid...and they will soon find out they're heading into dire straits of long-term vaccine side effects with every day that ticks away.

They were the victims of a mass mind-control operation called Mass Formation Psychosis. This was brought on by the talking heads at the UN/WHO/CDC/FDA, backed up by politicians, and spellbound by the media.

CHAPTER 5F

THE VACCINE

"Pharma has 80 COVID vaccines in development, but Gates & Fauci pushed Moderna's "Frankenstein jab" to the front of the line.

Scientists & ethicists are sounding alarms...

The vaccine uses a new, untested, and very controversial experimental mRNA technology that Gates has backed for over a decade.

Instead of injecting an antigen & adjuvant as with traditional vaccines, Moderna plugs a small piece of coronavirus genetic code into human cells, altering DNA throughout the human body and reprograming our cells to produce antibodies to fight the virus.

MRNA vaccines are a form of genetic engineering called "germ line gene editing". <u>Moderna's genetic alterations are passed down to future generations.</u>

In January, The Geneva Statement (the world's leading ethicists and scientists) called for an end to this kind of experimentation.

Moderna has never brought a product to market, proceeded through clinical trials, or had a vaccine approved by FDA.

Despite Gates' investments, the company, was teetering on bankruptcy with $1.5 billion debt before COVID.

Fauci's support won the company an astonishing $483 million in federal funds to accelerate development.

Dr. Joseph Bolen, <u>Moderna's former R&D Chief</u>, expressed shock at Fauci's bet. "I don't know what their thinking was", he told CNN, "When I read that, I was pretty amazed".

Moderna and Fauci launched federally-funded human trials on March 3rd, 2020 in Seattle.

Dr. Peter Hotez warns of potentially fatal consequences from skipping animal studies. "If there is immune enhancement in animals, that's a show-stopper".

Dr. Suhab Siddiqi, <u>Moderna's Ex-Director of Chemistry</u>, told CNN, "I would not let the [vaccine] be injected in my body. I would demand: Where is the toxicity data?"

Former NIH Scientist Dr. Judy Mikovits says its criminal to test mRNA vaccines on humans. "MRNA can cause cancers and other dire harms that don't surface for years."

-Robert F. Kennedy Jr, 5/2/20 on Instagram

CNN put the ex-Moderna doc on the mic, and he spoke a dire warning, and the people were none the wiser because of Goebbel's quote. If they were watching, his words went in one ear and right out the other because the words weren't registering. All the people understood at the time was what had been pounded into their heads: Deadly Pandemic and ~~Climate Change~~ Safe and Effective.

Excess deaths are steadily rising in the first-world countries as I edit this book in mid-2023, with both Australia and New Zealand now reporting huge spikes in excess deaths of their population. New Zealand was reporting numbers that hadn't been seen since the people they were losing during World War II!

"Attack Vaccines" have been in the Illuminati's arsenal for many decades at this point. And they kept ratcheting it up via the CDC Childhood Vaccine Schedule until we got to Endgame.

Surely Big Pharma was only looking out for our best interests... right? Their motives had nothing to do with agendas or money...right?

Let me tell you a story about a little company named Merck.

You probably have heard of Merck? This is the Merck that kept Vioxx on the market after they knew it was killing people in order to maximize profits before they pulled it. Yeah, **THAT** Merck! Their lawyers must have worked up a formula to figure out how much liability they could withstand before they started losing money by keeping Vioxx on the market. Turns out the number was 55,000 human deaths they could be sued over before Vioxx would become unprofitable and at that point they took it off the market in September 2004.

It seems very likely, near certain in fact, if you give a corrupt entity like Merck or Pfizer a green light to turn a highly profitable drug loose on a trusting, naive population with zero liability you better believe they're going to 'rush' an experimental vaccine out there even if it will kill you.

Pfizer ended up making billions in profits for 2021 and 2022, and why wouldn't they? The Feds bankrolled the 'research' for an emergency Covid vaccine and then Pfizer and the rest turned around and SOLD it back to the Feds to give away for "free"...HA!

Once a drug gets FDA approval, even Emergency Use Authorization as the Covid vaccines, they are eligible to be covered by Medicare. This is part of the gigantic scam of Big Pharma. They are inventing drugs that barely work, don't work at all, or outright kill you and paying off the FDA to approve them...making these scams eligible for Medicare for the elderly!!

And guess what? Pfizer stock is the 6th most popular stock for our congressmen and women to own, and Johnson and Johnson is the 7th!

WTH!!!

Our corrupt Congress-creatures made money off the plannedemic!

Literal murder money right into their filthy, corrupt pockets!!

What Merck did with Vioxx pales in comparison to what just happened.

50,000 lives is a drop in the bucket compared to the billions that took an mRNA injection and now have a ticking time bomb pulsing through their veins.

And we paid for it all.

Whether through the government we fund that gave hundreds of millions of dollars to Big Pharma to "find a covid vaccine immediately", the Big Pharma vaccines and medicines we buy or are indirectly bought through our health insurance premiums, or the lawsuits settled. We paid for it. All that money flying around amongst diabolical people who help themselves to our detriment comes from us, the citizens of the USA and the world.

We. Are. Being. Waged. War. Upon.

The United States spends the most money on healthcare in the world, over $4 trillion or so annually, and we have the worst SIDS (Sudden Infant Death Syndrome) rate in the world.

How is that even possible???

We already know…right, friend? The USA is in the crosshairs of the Illuminati more than any other country because the UN can't rise until we fall…fact!

The current vaccine schedule sent out by the CDC to the citizens of the United States of America consists of approximately **25** injections of biohazardous vaccines ***before age 1***, not including the now-recommended

Covid vaccine series and booster! And many more after age 1 all the way up to age 18....and beyond!

That's right: **25 or more separate injections before age 1** and the first one, Hepatitis B, comes **within minutes or hours of being born**. And you'd never guess who is the primary supplier of the Hep B injections...

Merck.

Hepatitis B is a disease of intravenous drug users who are shooting up drugs like heroin and meth with contaminated needles.

Now, I'm not a brain surgeon, but I think I can safely assume my one-day old newborn is not going to be shooting up drugs and is not at risk from Hepatitis B...and doesn't need this shot now or ever!

Coming out of the womb into this world was a shock enough and within minutes they are injecting the baby with a hep b vaccine full of too many poisons to list here!

Merck invented the first Hep B vac and when the drug addicts didn't come pounding down their door to buy their vaccine...good ol' Merck came for our kids and lobbied (bribed) the CDC to add it the kids vaccine schedule!!

We have a bunch of psychopath eugenicists in charge of our nation's healthcare!!!

After all the chips have fallen and the truth comes out, the depopulation shots will have been *"for our own good to save the world from 'climate change.' Mankind had to be culled back down to a non-threatening number."*

When the FDA voted to give Emergency Use Authorization for Pfizer's vaccine to be administered to 5–11-year-olds, panelist Dr. Eric Rubin said **"We're never going to learn about how safe the vaccine is until we start giving it"**.

How's THAT for a warning not to get your kids the shot!!!!

And then there's this to make note of I came across during the fray:

From a bulletin dated June 30, 2021 from OSHA entitled: COVID-19: Frequently Asked Questions/Occupational Safety and Health Administration.

Question: Are adverse reactions to the COVID-19 vaccine recordable on the OSHA recordkeeping log?

Answer: DOL and OSHA, as well as other federal agencies, are working diligently to encourage COVID-19 vaccinations. OSHA does not wish to have any appearance of discouraging workers from receiving COVID-19 vaccination, and also does not wish to disincentive employers' vaccination efforts. As a result, OSHA will not enforce 29 CFR 1904's recording requirements to require any employers to record worker side effects from COVID-19 vaccination through <u>May 2022</u>. We will reevaluate the agency's position at that time to determine the best course of action moving forward.

OSHA (the feds) were admittedly HIDING incredibly important information about the number of vaccine injuries!!

This is the same OSHA that was charged by Biden with enforcing his illegal mandatory vaccine mandate that any company with over 100 employees must vax all of them!

This was eventually struck down by the courts but Biden literally ordered companies to adhere to his mandate while it was on appeal!!!! That's purely a dick move!!! UGGHHH!!!

Biden condemned millions who wouldn't have otherwise gotten the jab to save their job but were coerced to. I can't blame them for obeying, it looked like the economy was going to go over the cliff at the time.

Among those people who did do their research, and are experts in their respected professions, and have seen first-hand the side effects of the jabs, and lost their jobs/livelihoods for refusing these jabs were doctors, nurses, firemen, police, medics…many, many against themselves and others taking these mysterious vaccines.

If we were really in an (alleged) deadly pandemic, do you think they would have been firing nurses and doctors and emergency personnel??? Especially ones who already made it just fine through 2020 without a jab or two??? Or those who had the 'rona and had the antibodies against it?

Forced medical experimentation (mandatory experimental vaccines) on the general public by one's government is illegal, unethical, immoral, and tyrannical. Period. There is a reason there is a Nuremburg Code in existence…we've been through this before less than 100 years ago!

And here's another rando for you:

It came out (quietly) that Pfizer added tromethamine, a blood-stabilizer, to the vaccines right as they were green-lighted to start injecting 5-11 year old kids by the FDA on October 29, 2021. I'm assuming this was for the heart issues that were making themselves known at the time.

So…they changed the formula for **_children_** and didn't do any clinical trials for safety…perfect.

Normally, in a sane world, these kinds of changes to a vaccine, let alone the vaccines themselves, take many years of testing to ensure "safety," which is why all vaccines before the covid vaccine were the slow-kill-class. These new Covid vaccines are designed to kill and maim within years, not decades.

Here is the wording of the requested change, which can be found in a PDF by searching for "fda gov 153447 media pdf":

"Authorization is being requested for a modified formulation of the Pfizer-BioNTech COVID-19 Vaccine. Each dose of this formulation contains 10 µg of a nucleoside-modified messenger RNA (mRNA) encoding the viral spike (S) glycoprotein of SARS-CoV-2 that is formulated in lipid particles and supplied as a frozen suspension in multiple dose vials.

To provide a vaccine with an improved stability profile, the Pfizer-BioNTech COVID-19 Vaccine for use in children 5-11 years of age uses tromethamine (Tris) buffer instead of the phosphatebuffered saline (PBS) as used in the previous formulation and excludes sodium chloride and potassium chloride."

I also found this while BRIEFLY snooping other items in this PDF...

"...Although some cases of vaccine-associated myocarditis/pericarditis have required intensive care support, available data from short-term follow-up suggest that **most** individuals have had resolution of **symptoms** with **conservative management.** Information is not yet available about potential **long-term sequelae** and outcomes in affected individuals, **OR (!!!)** whether the vaccine might be associated initially with subclinical myocarditis (and if so, what are the **long-term sequelae**). *A mechanism of action by which the vaccine could cause myocarditis and pericarditis has not been established. Myocarditis and pericarditis were added as important identified risks in the PVP and included in the Warnings sections of the vaccine Fact Sheets and Prescribing Information.* The Sponsor is conducting additional post-authorization/post-marketing studies to assess known serious risks of myocarditis and pericarditis as well as to identify an unexpected serious risk of subclinical myocarditis....

What they are saying here is that when people are initially injured by the vaccine and come down with heart problems, they are then forced onto expensive heart medications with side effects of their own...for which more drugs will be prescribed!!

They are also flat out admitting that they have no information about long-term side effects when it comes to heart issues but, hey, they put it right in the vaccine Fact Sheets and Prescribing Information and if you didn't request to see these, read them, and understand them, that's on you, bud.

If you are a new reader of mine who took the mRNA vaccine in particular, you should immediately go in for a 'd-dimer' test, which tests for the formation/presence of small blood clots---the beginning of the side effects of massive blood clots that will kill you eventually. They can then administer blood thinners or whatever they can do for you. I'm pulling for you, friend.

For all to investigate further the excess death numbers now happening worldwide, type into <duckduckgo> "statistics excess death population 2021 2022 2023"

Another good website to know and pass on to those you know who were vaccinated, and what their outlook may be, is "howbadismybatch". This site gives out how many people died or were maimed from any particular batch, in any particular area.

I have heard that if you plug in all the numbers, the scuttlebutt is that the most deadly batches were sent to 'Red' areas of the USA, that is, the Conservative states/counties.

I wouldn't doubt it.

CHAPTER 6

THE SENTINELS OF TRUTH

How many times during the plannedemic did the controlled media bellow "trust the science" but no names of trusted, non-compromised scientists and researchers were given?

The credible people I'm listing in this next chapter run circles around Fauci because they don't have ulterior motives and spoke the brutal, honest truth.

In fact, these are arguably the doctors and scientists with the best credibility in the entire world for speaking out about the plannedemic. One of them invented the mRNA technology used in the Pfizer/Moderna shots, and another invented the PCR test, for which he won a Nobel Prize, which was used to "authenticate" the non-pandemic.

By their bold actions they shouldn't even have to ask us to stand up with them against the obvious false flag to trigger the Great Reset... to back them up...that they are indeed in the right, and in the fight for humanity.

They didn't have to ask. We will stand with them against evil.

C'mon. Let's go meet them.

CHAPTER 6A

ROBERT F. KENNEDY JR.

Yes, Robert F. Kennedy Jr. is the son of Robert (Bobby) Kennedy who was assassinated in the 1960s as his brother was, President John F. Kennedy.

If his last name wasn't Kennedy, the mainstream media would have ripped him to pieces long ago as a quack conspiracy theorist but he has vastly too much credibility to bring attention to him, so instead they avoid him like the plague to try and prevent his words and warnings from gaining traction.

Too late. Now he's running for President!! This is going to get interesting, folks.

RFK Jr. is a notable environmental attorney who has now founded and heads Children's Health Defense, primarily an organization to raise awareness of the dangers of vaccines, and now especially the covid vaccines. I subscribe to their online newsletter and I recommend you do also. Always good links from there weekly to pass around to others.

This here below is an excerpt from an interview he did that I found on the Children's Health Defense website, an affirmation of his heart and character. You better believe he'd never be seen at Epstein Island!!

This is only about ¼ of the interview and would recommend reading the rest as RFK Jr. is going after the corrupt CDC/Fauci like a lion!

"Environmental and humanitarian legend RFK, Jr., mainstream media, and the very corrupt CDC"
Interview by Rita Shreffler, CHD Director of Advocacy & Outreach

"For over three decades, Robert F. Kennedy, Jr. has been one of the world's leading environmental advocates. He is the founder of Waterkeeper Alliance, the umbrella group for 300 local waterkeeper organizations, in 34 countries, that track down and sue polluters. Under his leadership, Waterkeeper has grown to become the world's largest clean water advocacy organization.

Around 2005, parents of vaccine-injured children began encountering Mr. Kennedy's speeches and writings about the toxic mercury-based preservative thimerosal. They embraced new hope that this environmental champion would finally expose the truth about vaccine injury and win justice for injured children. Kennedy is known for his fierce and relentless brand of environmental activism and his advocacy for transparent government and rigorous science. He is now applying his tenacious energies and sophisticated strategies to exposing the fraud and corruption within the CDC and the pharmaceutical industry. Last month, he launched his new non-profit, the Children's Health Defense, with vaccine safety advocates Lyn Redwood and Laura Bono, legends themselves among parents of vaccine-injured children. Autism File executive editor Rita Shreffler spoke with Mr. Kennedy about CDC corruption, pharmaceutical industry greed, media malpractice, and his vision for the Children's Health Defense.

Rita Shreffler: How did you first get involved in the autism/vaccine controversy?

Robert F. Kennedy: I was dragged kicking and screaming into this brawl. By the early 2000s, I was fighting multiple lawsuits on behalf of Riverkeeper and Waterkeeper against coal-fired power plants. I was touring the country speaking about, among other things, the dangers of mercury emissions, which, by then, had contaminated virtually every fresh water fish in America. Following many of these appearances, mothers would approach me. Their tone was always respectful but mildly scolding. They said that if I was serious about eliminating the perils of mercury, I needed to look at thimerosal. Vaccines, they claimed, were the biggest vector for mercury exposure in children. I really didn't want to get involved because vaccines were pretty remote from my wheelhouse. I'd always been pro-vaccine. I had all my kids vaccinated and got my annual flu shot every year. But, I was impressed by these women. Many of them were professionals: doctors, lawyers, scientists, nurses and pharmacists. They were overwhelmingly solid, well-educated, extraordinarily well-informed, rational and persuasive.

RS: Was there a particular one of these mothers who finally got you to take the bait?

RFK: Yeah, my brother Max's wife, Vicky Strauss Kennedy, introduced me to a psychologist named Sarah Bridges. Her son Porter was vaccine-injured and later diagnosed with autism. After an eight-year legal battle, she had finally received compensation from the vaccine court, which acknowledged that Porter got his autism, seizures and brain damage from thimerosal and pertussis vaccines. She persuaded me to start looking into the science.

RS: That was a daunting request!

RKF: I have always loved science and I'm comfortable reading it. By then, I'd handled many hundreds of environmental cases. Almost all of them involved scientific controversies. When I started reading about thimerosal, I was dumbstruck by the gulf between the scientific reality and the media consensus. All the network news anchors and television doctors were assuring the public that there was not a single study that suggested thimerosal was unsafe or that it could cause autism. After a short time on PubMed, I'd identified many dozens of studies suggesting that thimerosal causes autism and a rich library of peer-reviewed literature—over 400 published studies—attesting to its deadly toxicity and its causal connection to a long inventory of neurological injuries and organ damage.

RS: What do we know about thimerosal safety testing?

RFK: First of all, vaccines are not subject to the safety rigors undergone by other pharmaceuticals in the FDA approval process. There are no large scale, double-blind, placebo-controlled studies. And, in the one 1930 human study of thimerosal that predated its use in vaccines, all the subjects injected with thimerosal died. In 2004, an FDA official acknowledged in testimony before a Congressional committee, that no government or privately funded study has ever demonstrated thimerosal's safety. On the other hand, there is plenty of science suggesting that thimerosal is NOT safe. Several hundred studies available on PubMed link thimerosal exposure to the neurodevelopmental and immune system diseases that are now epidemic in the generation of American children born after the CDC dramatically increased childhood thimerosal exposure starting in 1988. My book, Thimerosal— Let the Science Speak, summarizes these studies. The scientific literature inculpates increased thimerosal exposure as a culprit in the explosion of

ADD, ADHD, speech delay, narcolepsy, SIDS, ASD, seizure disorder, tics and anaphylaxis, including asthma and food allergies. According to the CDC, one in six American children—the so called "thimerosal generation"—now suffers from a developmental disability. We have published a compendium of 80 published, peer-reviewed studies that strongly suggest a link between thimerosal exposure and autism.

RS: The CDC started adding to the vaccine schedule in the late 1980s and all these diseases, including autism, began spiking among kids in the mid-1990s. That's when parents started seeing perfectly healthy children regress into autism after receiving their vaccines.

RFK: Yeah. A rising chorus of complaints from parents and pediatricians linked the new thimerosal-heavy vaccine schedule to an explosion in autism. In response, the CDC, in 1999, commissioned an in-house Belgian researcher, Thomas Verstraeten, to study the Vaccine Safety Datalink, the largest American repository of childhood vaccine and health records, collected by HMOs. The HMO data clearly showed that the massive mercury doses in the newly expanded vaccine schedule were causing runaway epidemics of neurological disorders— ADD, ADHD, speech delay, sleep disorders, tics and autism among America's children. Verstraeten's original analysis of those datasets found that thimerosal exposures increased autism risk by 760%. The CDC now knew the cause of the autism epidemic.

RS: How did the CDC react to the revelations in the Verstraeten study?

RFK: The vaccine branch called an emergency meeting of regulators from WHO, FDA, vaccine industry stakeholders and the American Academy of Pediatrics at the Simpsonwood Conferences and Retreat Center in Norcross, Georgia. They reportedly held the meeting off the CDC campus to shield the deliberations from freedom of information requests. During a frantic two-day debate, that group decided to embargo Verstraeten's study. The CDC then pushed Verstraeten aside and assembled a team of industry and CDC scientists to rework the study using dodgey statistical devices to make the autism signal disappear. After four increasingly deceptive iterations, that team succeeded in eliminating the signal linking thimerosal with autism and a half dozen other neurodevelopmental disorders. The CDC published that version and told the public that thimerosal was safe. When parents asked to see the raw data, the CDC claimed that it had somehow "lost" all the raw data so that no independent group could check this result.

RS: Right, that's when the CDC went into the business of creating its notorious phony epidemiological studies?

RFK: Exactly. Over the next two years, the CDC worked with the pharmaceutical industry to gin up seven epidemiological studies that purport to exculpate thimerosal from causing the autism epidemic. None of these studies pretend to be safety studies. Each of them simply looked for the presence of a small number of designated diseases in specific populations exposed to thimerosal. All of them are fatally flawed due to improper methodologies or deliberate fraud. Nevertheless, these are the studies that the CDC lists on its website—and that its spokespeople regularly cite—to defend mercury in vaccines. It's worth noting that the CDC itself has so little faith in these studies that it derailed a scheduled 2012 review of their underlying science by the Institute of Medicine (IOM) and killed a 2006 review of thimerosal safety by the National Toxicology Program. Under CDC pressure, the Institute of Medicine made the astonishing declaration, in 2004, that, based on those seven flawed studies, the science was settled and no new studies on the causative relationship between thimerosal and autism should be undertaken or funded. That declaration effectively cut off support for any scientist who wants to investigate the link.

RS: The CDC touts those seven epidemiological studies across the globe as evidence of thimerosal safety.

RFK: Yes, and CDC and IOM officials left behind a very troubling email trail that makes it clear that those studies were deliberately manufactured to exonerate thimerosal. By the time I came across them, I was accustomed to dissecting research papers and spotting junk science. In my line, we call it "tobacco science" and the hired guns who generate it "biostitutes". The CDC's primary data manager on its widely touted Danish studies was a notorious con man and professional biostitute named Poul Thorsen, who actually pocketed the million dollars the CDC paid him to do the research. He is currently under indictment on 22 counts of wire fraud and money laundering by the U.S. Justice Department and is the star of the OIG's Most Wanted List. Thorsen is on the run from the FBI in Europe. Nevertheless, the CDC still uses Thorsen's studies as proof of thimerosal safety...."

Well, I think it's safe to say that Kennedy is solidly on our side.

Thank you, Mr. Kennedy, for what you are doing, putting your life in danger tangling with the Deep State that cost your uncle and father their lives.

"Vaccines, for Bill Gates, are a strategic philanthropy that feeds his many vaccine-related businesses (including Microsoft's ambition to control a global vac ID enterprise) and gives him dictatorial control over global health policy—the spear tip of corporate neo-imperialism"

-Robert F. Kennedy Jr.

There are millions of people waking up to the vaccine agenda, including a handful of Hollywood stars, and even some whose kids have been vaccine injured including Robert DeNiro. In fact, DeNiro and Kennedy have teamed up to offer $100,000 to anyone who could conclusively prove that vaccines are safe!!

Kennedy just came out with a book that has gone bestseller all over the place, called 'The Real Anthony Fauci'.

I haven't read it yet but I've heard what's in it and if you want to know even more crazy, evil stuff about Fauci, Gates and the rest than I've already told you then you should get this book and read it! I'm sure it will end up in my library soon.

(It did.)

CHAPTER 6B

DR. ROBERT MALONE

You might already know that Dr. Malone is the inventor of the mRNA technology currently deployed against humanity in the Moderna and Pfizer jabs…but he's no bad guy to be sure.

Doc Malone didn't pull any punches when the 'get vaccinated' campaign was in high gear in 2021. He flat out told everyone that would listen that the mRNA vaccines are a horrible risk to humanity and to stop administering them immediately. He was kicked off Twitter at the time for repeating this…over and over. And over. He was also marginalized as a kook by the mainstream media.

The inventor of the mRNA vaccine that allegedly saved humanity was booted off Twitter for vaccine misinformation…for speaking out against **HIS OWN CREATION!**

Before this happened, Malone went on his LinkedIn and sent out a letter to every professional health worker he could, warning them about the vaccine and was booted off there also.

In June 2021 Dr. Malone released a 3-hour video online telling people not to get the mRNA vaccines.

Dr. Robert Malone is very clearly the inventor of the mRNA technology and the media will barely and begrudgingly acknowledge that fact because HE WAS AGAINST THE COVID VACCINES!!!

Here are excerpts from a Deep State publication called 'The Atlantic', dated August 21, 2021. This was the big NWO hit-piece on Dr. Robert Malone's credibility, the one that was often referenced by the mainstream media when they tried to downgrade him as a purveyor of misinformation.

((((((((((((*Robert Malone—a medical doctor and an infectious-disease researcher—recently suggested that the Pfizer and Moderna vaccines might actually make COVID-19 infections worse. He chuckled as he imagined Anthony Fauci announcing that the vaccination campaign was all a big mistake ("Oh darn, I was wrong!") and would need to be abandoned. When he floated that nightmare scenario during a recent podcast interview with Steve Bannon, both men seemed almost delighted at the prospect of public-health officials and pharmaceutical companies getting their comeuppance. "This is a catastrophe," Bannon declared, beaming at his guest. "You're hearing it from an individual who invented the mRNA [vaccine] and has dedicated his life to vaccines. He's the opposite of an anti-vaxxer."*

*Before going any further, let's be clear that the back-and-forth between Bannon and Malone was premised on misinformation. The vaccines have repeatedly been shown to help prevent symptomatic coronavirus infections and reduce their severity. Malone was riffing on a botched sentence in a USA Today article, one that was later deleted but not before being screenshotted and widely shared. That kind of overheated, spottily sourced conversation is par for the course on shows like Bannon's, which traffic in a set of claims that sound depressingly familiar: **<u>The vaccines cause more harm than experts are letting on; Fauci is a liar and possibly a fascist; and the mainstream news media is either shamelessly complicit or too stupid to figure out what's really going on.</u>***

In that alternate media universe, Robert Malone's star is ascendant. He started popping up on podcasts and cable news shows a few months ago, presented as a scientific expert, arguing that the approval process for the vaccines had been unwisely rushed. He told Tucker Carlson that the public doesn't have enough information to decide whether to get vaccinated. He told Glenn Beck that offering incentives for taking vaccines is unethical. He told Del Bigtree, an anti-vaccine activist who opposes common childhood inoculations, that there hadn't been sufficient research on how the vaccines might affect women's reproductive systems. On show after show, Malone, who has quickly amassed more than 200,000 Twitter followers, casts doubt on the safety of the vaccines while decrying what he sees as attempts to censor dissent.

Wherever he appears, Malone is billed as the inventor of mRNA vaccines. It's in his Twitter bio. "I literally invented mRNA technology when I was 28," says Malone, who is now 61. If that's true—or, more to the point, if Malone believes it to be true—then you might expect him to be championing a very different message in his media appearances. According to one recent study, the innovation for which he claims to be responsible has already saved hundreds of thousands of lives in the United States alone; there's talk that it may soon lead to a round of Nobel Prizes. It's the kind of validation that few scientists in history have ever received. Yet instead of taking a victory lap, **_Malone has emerged as one of the most vocal critics of his own alleged accomplishment_**. He's sowed doubt about the Pfizer and Moderna vaccines on pretty much any podcast or YouTube channel that will have him.

Why is the self-described inventor of the mRNA vaccines working so hard to undermine them?

143

Whether Malone really came up with mRNA vaccines is a question probably best left to Swedish prize committees, but you could make a case for his involvement. When I called Malone at his 50-acre horse farm in Virginia, he directed me to a 6,000-word essay written by his wife, Jill, that lays out why he believes himself to be the primary discoverer. "This is a story about academic and commercial avarice," it begins. The document's tone is pointed, and at times lapses into all-caps fury. She frames her husband as a genius scientist who is "largely unknown by the scientific establishment because of abuses by individuals to secure their own place in the history books."

The abridged version is that when Malone was a graduate student in biology in the late 1980s at the Salk Institute for Biological Studies, he injected genetic material—DNA and RNA—into the cells of mice in hopes of creating a new kind of vaccine. He was the first author on a 1989 paper demonstrating how RNA could be delivered into cells using lipids, which are basically tiny globules of fat, and a co-author on a 1990 Science paper showing that if you inject pure RNA or DNA into mouse muscle cells, it can lead to the transcription of new proteins. If the same approach worked for human cells, the latter paper said in its conclusion, this technology "may provide alternative approaches to vaccine development."

These two studies do indeed represent seminal work in the field of gene transfer, according to Rein Verbeke, a postdoctoral fellow at Ghent University, in Belgium, and the lead author of a 2019 history of mRNA-vaccine development. (Indeed, Malone's studies are the first two references in Verbeke's paper, out of 224 in total.) *Verbeke told me he believes that Malone and his co-authors "sparked for the first time the hope that mRNA could have potential as a new drug class," though he also notes that "the achievement of the mRNA vaccines of today is the accomplishment of a lot of collaborative efforts."*

Malone says he deserves credit for more than just sparking hope. He dropped out of graduate school in 1988, just short of his Ph.D., and went to work at a pharmaceutical company called Vical. Now he claims that both the Salk Institute and Vical profited from his work and essentially prevented him from further pursuing his research. (A Salk Institute spokesperson said that nothing in the institute's records substantiates Malone's allegations. The biotech company into which Vical was merged, Brickell, did not respond to requests for comment.) To say that Malone remains bitter over this perceived mistreatment doesn't do justice to his sense of aggrievement. He calls what happened to him "intellectual rape."

One target of Malone's ire, the biochemist Katalin Karikó, has been featured in multiple news stories as an mRNA-vaccine pioneer. CNN called her work "the basis of the Covid-19 vaccine" while a New York Times headline said she had "helped shield the world from the coronavirus." None of those stories mentioned Malone. "I've been written out of the history," he has said. "It's all about Kati." Karikó shared with me an email that Malone sent her in June, accusing her of feeding reporters bogus information and inflating her own accomplishments. "This is not going to end well," Malone's message says.

Karikó replied that she hadn't told anyone that she is the inventor of mRNA vaccines and that "many many scientists" contributed to their success. "I have never claimed more than discovering a way to make RNA less inflammatory," she wrote to him. She told me that Malone referred to himself in an email as her "mentor" and "coach," though she says they've met in person only once, in 1997, when he invited her to give a talk. It's Malone, according to Karikó, who has been overstating his accomplishments. There are "hundreds of scientists who contributed more to mRNA vaccines than he did."

Malone insists that his warning to Karikó that "this is not going to end well" was not intended as a threat. Instead, he says, he was suggesting that her exaggerations would soon be exposed. Malone views Karikó as yet another scientist standing on his shoulders and collecting plaudits that should go to him. Others have been rewarded handsomely for their work on mRNA vaccines, he says. (Karikó is a senior vice president at BioNTech, which partnered with Pfizer to create the first COVID-19 vaccine to be authorized for use last year.) Malone is not exactly living on the streets: In addition to being a medical doctor, he has served as a vaccine consultant for pharmaceutical companies....

....Malone may keep company with vaccine skeptics, but he insists he is not one himself. His objections to the Pfizer and Moderna shots have to do mostly with their expedited approval process and with the government's system for tracking adverse reactions. Speaking as a doctor, he would probably recommend their use only for those at highest risk from COVID-19. Everyone else should be wary, he told me, and those under 18 should be excluded entirely. (A June 23 statement from more than a dozen public-health organizations and agencies strongly encouraged all eligible people 12 and older to get vaccinated, because the benefits "far outweigh any harm.") Malone is also frustrated that, as he sees it, complaints about side effects are being ignored or censored in the nationwide push to increase vaccination rates.

*You might very well walk away with the skewed sense, after hearing Malone speak or reading his posts, **that there is a far-reaching COVID-19 cover-up and that the real threat is the vaccine rather than the virus**. I've listened to hours of Malone's interviews and read through the many pages of documents he's posted. He is a knowledgeable scientist with a knack for lucid explanation. It doesn't hurt that he looks the part with his neatly trimmed white beard, or that he has a voice that would be well suited for a meditation app. Malone is not a subscriber to the more out-there conspiracy theories regarding COVID-19 vaccines—he doesn't, for instance, think Bill Gates has snuck microchips into* syringes—and he sometimes pushes back gently when hosts like Bigtree or Beck drift into more ludicrous territory.

And yet he does routinely slip into speculation that turns out to be misleading or, as in the segment on Bannon's show, plainly false. For instance, he recently tweeted that, according to an unnamed "Israeli scientist," **_Pfizer and the Israeli government have an agreement not to release information about adverse effects for 10 years_**, which is hard to believe given that the country's health ministry has already warned of a link between the Pfizer shot and rare cases of myocarditis. Malone's LinkedIn account has twice been suspended for supposedly spreading misinformation.

His concerns are personal, too. Malone contracted COVID-19 in February 2020, and later got the Moderna vaccine in hopes that it would alleviate his long-haul symptoms. Now he believes the injections made his symptoms worse: He still has a cough and is dealing with hypertension and reduced stamina, among other maladies. "My body will never be the same," he told me. In media appearances, he often notes that he has colleagues in the government and at universities who agree with him and are privately cheering him on…

It's only in the curious world of fringe media that Malone has found the platform, and the recognition, he's sought for so long. He talks to hosts who aren't going to question whether he's the brains behind the Pfizer and Moderna shots. They're not going to quibble over whether credit should be shared with co-authors, or talk about how science is like a relay race, or point out that, absent the hard work of brilliant researchers who came before and after Malone, there would be no vaccine. He's an upgrade over their typical guest list of chiropractors and naturopaths, and they're perfectly happy to address him by the title he believes he's earned: inventor of the mRNA vaccines.

The irony is that, to the audiences who tune in to those shows, the vaccines are seen as a scourge rather than a godsend. No matter how nuanced Malone might try to be, or how many qualifiers he appends to his opinions, he is egging on vaccine hesitancy at a time when hospitals in the least-vaccinated parts of the country are struggling to cope with an influx of new COVID-19 patients. If you want proof of that, scroll through the many comments from his followers thanking him for confirming their fears. Malone has finally made his mark, by undermining confidence in the very vaccine he says wouldn't be possible without his genius. It's a victory, of sorts, but one that he and the rest of us may come to regret...)))))))))))))))))

I included all pertinent info from that Atlantic article, and there is not one place where the Atlantic specifically denies that Malone is the inventor of the mRNA technology and actually made a case for it IMHO.

When covid vaccinations were approved for children aged 5-11 on October 29, 2021, Dr. Malone put the following out there as a statement for public consumption, obviously this was never broadcast anywhere but alternative media:

"Before you inject your child, a decision that is irreversible, I wanted to let you know the scientific facts about this genetic vaccine, which is based on the mRNA vaccine technology I created.

There are three issues parents need to understand:

The first is that a viral gene will be injected into your children's cells. This gene forces your child's body to make toxic spike proteins. These proteins often cause permanent damage in children's critical organs, including:

Their brain and nervous system.

Their heart and blood vessels, including blood clots.

Their reproductive system.

This vaccine can trigger fundamental changes to their immune system.

The most alarming point about this is that once these damages have occurred, they are irreparable.

You can't fix the lesions within their brain.

You can't repair heart tissue scarring.

You can't repair a genetically reset immune system.

This vaccine can cause reproductive damage that could affect future generations of your family.

The second thing you need to know about is the fact that this novel technology has not been adequately tested.

We need at least 5 years of testing/research before we can really understand the risks.

Harms and risks from new medicines often become revealed many years later.

Ask yourself if you want your own child to be part of the most radical medical experiment in human history.

One final point: the reason they're giving you to vaccinate your child is a lie.

Your children represent no danger to their parents or grandparents.

It's actually the opposite. Their immunity, after getting covid, is critical to save your family if not the world from this disease.

In summary, there is no benefit for your children or your family to be vaccinating your children against the small risks of the virus, given the known health risks of the vaccine that as a parent, you and your children may have to live with for the rest of their lives.

The risk/benefit analysis isn't even close.

As a parent and grandparent, **my recommendation to you is to <u>resist and fight to protect your children.</u>"**

Couldn't agree with you more, doc. Thank you for selflessly putting your own life at risk to go public with your professional opinion as a doctor, and as the inventor of the mRNA technology.

CARY MULLIS

Cary Mullis is the Nobel Prize-winning inventor of the PCR test that was used to convince everyone we were in a deadly pandemic, which we weren't.

If you run the PCR test with enough cycles, it will give a positive reading on whatever you want it to. This is why the CDC has gradually dropped the number of recommended cycles lower and lower and has now finally admitted the tests are flawed and are moving away from them....

THIS WAS AFTER THEY BASED THEIR ENTIRE PANDEMIC-NARRATIVE ON THE ACCURACY OF THESE TESTS WHICH ENABLED THE IMPLEMENTATION OF THE FALSE FLAG PLANNEDEMIC!!

If Mullis was alive when this was going on he would have been screaming fraud from the rooftops as you'll see, but coincidentally enough he died on August 7, 2019 just weeks before the plannedemic kicked off.

Imagine that.

He was not a timid or shy man and not afraid to call people out. He has even publicly called out Fauci for his diabolical role in the AIDS epidemic!

Right off the bat, here's this from Mullis' Wikipedia page. Wikipedia is typically pro-NWO propaganda, but this serves our purpose on a couple fronts:

*"Kary Banks Mullis (December 28, 1944 – August 7, 2019) was an American biochemist. In recognition of his role in the invention of the polymerase chain reaction (PCR) technique, he shared the 1993 Nobel Prize in Chemistry with Michael Smith and was awarded the Japan Prize in the same year. PCR became a central technique in biochemistry and molecular biology, described by The New York Times as "highly original and significant, virtually dividing biology into the two epochs of before PCR and after PCR." Mullis attracted controversy for **denying humans' role in climate change...**"*

If you read the whole Wiki entry you will see exactly what I mean by pro-NWO propaganda as Mullis is lambasted as an eccentric loon with no credibility whereas the quote above shows that he does indeed have credibility and profoundly influenced the world of science...he literally changed it forever.

He was no fan of Fauci either...one more reason he wasn't allowed to live to see the dawn of the plannedemic only 3 months after his death. He was a freethinker and vocally anti-Deep State, and especially anti-Fauci!

This is a quote right from Mullis that I watched with my own eyes and heard personally in an interview from 1996 when the AIDS epidemic was big news. You might still be able to find this interview to verify for yourself and others, so don't let anyone tell you otherwise that this quote is untrue. Try bitchute, they have everything that YouTube has banned:

*"**What is it about humanity that wants to go through all the details and stuff...guys like Fauci get up there and start talking...he doesn't know***

*anything really about anything and I'd say that to his face: **NOTHING.*** *The man thinks you can take a blood sample and stick it in an electron microscope and if it's got a virus in there you'll know it. He doesn't understand electron microscopy and he doesn't understand medicine and he should not be in the position like he's in. Most of those guys up there on the top are just total administrative people and they don't know anything about what's going on in the body. Those guys have got an agenda that is not what we would like them to have, being that we pay for them to take care of our health. They have a personal kind of agenda, they make up their own rules as they go, they change them when they want to...and they smugly...like Tony Fauci does not mind going on television in front of the people who pay his salary and lie directly in the camera..."*

Thank you for calling out Fauci a quarter-century ago, Mr. Mullis. Your words regarding him still ring true today, and were a disturbing harbinger of things to come.

RIP

MICHAEL YEADON

Dr. Yeadon is quite an interesting guy. When you dig into him you will find he's highly intelligent, a savvy businessman, and likes to speak his mind publicly about what he thinks of the plannedemic, the virus, the lockdowns, and the vaccines.

He was a higher-up, "company man" for Pfizer (!) for 16 years, eventually becoming the chief scientist and vice-president of the allergy and respiratory research division.

Pfizer decided to eliminate the division Yeadon was in, and he knew what would happen to his and others research: it would be mothballed and lost forever.

Yeadon and 3 others ended up founding a biotech out of their salvaged research and with backing from Pfizer and others, built it into a company called Ziarco that was ultimately sold to Novartis in 2017 for hundreds of millions of dollars.

There's a fantastic article I found about Yeadon and Ziarco on Deep-State-stalwart Fortune's website from 2017 before all this pandemic-BS was around.

Search for "Turning Pfizer Discards Into Novartis Gold: The Story Of Ziarco"

As one of the founders, Yeadon's initial Class A stock holdings would have been worth a significant amount in the millions when Ziarco was bought out such that he didn't have to work anymore and spent a lot of time giving his opinion about what was going on with the plannedemic during the craziness of it all.

Lucky us.

What he has stated publicly is right in line with what we already know: Covid 19 was a depopulation exercise.

His various viewpoints are to be taken extremely seriously, and we will get to them.

First lets quickly look at those who tried to shout his fact-based, rational statements down so the sheep didn't go wandering off down some radical rabbit hole that might cause them to cut their bonds and rebel against what was planned for us through the injections.

This sucker-punch courtesy of (not) your friend and mine, Wikipedia:

Michael Yeadon is a British anti-vaccine activist and retired pharmacologist who attracted media attention for making false or unfounded claims about the COVID-19 pandemic and the safety of COVID-19 vaccines. The Times has described him as "a hero of Covid conspiracy theorists "and "a key figure in the antivax movement". He previously served as the chief scientist and vice-president of the allergy and respiratory research division of the drug company Pfizer, and is the co-founder and former CEO of the biotechnology company Ziarco...

...When Pfizer closed its Kent research facility in 2011. Yeadon, who had not worked with vaccines, then left Pfizer and with three colleagues founded the biotechnology company Ziarco, which was later sold to Novartis for $325 million in 2017...

...Yeadon falsely claimed that the COVID-19 pandemic in the United Kingdom was "effectively over" in October 2020, that there would be no

"second wave" of infections, and that healthy people could not spread the SARS-CoV-2 virus. He has claimed without evidence that COVID-19 vaccines were unnecessary, unsafe, and could cause infertility in women. In a letter to the European Medicines Agency, Yeadon and the German physician Wolfgang Wodarg called for all vaccine trials to be stopped, falsely suggesting that mRNA vaccines could target the syncytin-1 protein needed for placenta formation. In an interview with political strategist Steve Bannon, Yeadon falsely asserted that children were "50 times more likely to be killed by the COVID vaccines than the virus itself", citing a high number of events following COVID-19 vaccination reported on the Vaccine Adverse Event Reporting System (VAERS) database. The US Centers for Disease Control, which operates the database, cautions that such reports are not verified and do not prove that vaccines caused any given adverse event. Yeadon has also discouraged COVID-19 lockdowns and the use of face masks despite evidence for their effectiveness. He has alleged that the vaccines cause recipients to become magnetic. Several of Yeadon's claims have been amplified on social media...

Let's do one more Deep State cheap-shot hit-piece, these excerpts are from Reuters in March 18, 2021, **"The ex-Pfizer scientist who became an anti-vax hero":**

"Michael Yeadon was a scientific researcher and vice president at drugs giant Pfizer Inc. He co-founded a successful biotech. Then his career took an unexpected turn.

Late last year, a semi-retired British scientist co-authored a petition to Europe's medicines regulator. The petitioners made a bold demand: Halt COVID-19 vaccine clinical trials.

Even bolder was their argument for doing so: They speculated, without providing evidence, that the vaccines could cause infertility in women.

The document appeared on a German website on Dec.1. Scientists denounced the theory. Regulators weren't swayed, either: Weeks later, the European Medicines Agency approved the European Union's first COVID-19 shot, co-developed by Pfizer Inc. But damage was already done.

Social media quickly spread exaggerated claims that COVID-19 jabs cause female infertility. Within weeks, doctors and nurses in Britain began reporting that concerned women were asking them whether it was true, according to the Royal College of Obstetricians & Gynecologists. In January, a survey by the Kaiser Family Foundation (KFF), a non-profit organization, found that 13% of unvaccinated people in the United States had heard that "COVID-19 vaccines have been shown to cause infertility."

What gave the debunked claim credibility was that one of the petition's co-authors, Michael Yeadon, wasn't just any scientist. The 60-year-old is a former vice president of Pfizer, where he spent 16 years as an allergy and respiratory researcher. He later co-founded a biotech firm that the Swiss drugmaker Novartis purchased for at least $325 million.

In recent months, Yeadon (pronounced Yee-don) has emerged as an unlikely hero of the so-called anti-vaxxers, whose adherents question the safety of many vaccines, including for the coronavirus. The anti-vaxxer movement has amplified Yeadon's skeptical views about COVID-19 vaccines and tests, government-mandated lockdowns and the arc of the pandemic. Yeadon has said he personally doesn't oppose the use of all vaccines. But many health experts and government officials worry that opinions like his fuel vaccine hesitancy – a reluctance or refusal to be vaccinated – that could prolong the pandemic. COVID-19 has already killed more than 2.6 million people worldwide.

"These claims are false, dangerous and deeply irresponsible," said a spokesman for Britain's Department of Health & Social Care, when

asked about Yeadon's views. "COVID-19 vaccines are the best way to protect people from coronavirus and will save thousands of lives."

On January 17, 2022, Dr. Yeadon did an interview with Planet Lockdown and put everything on his mind into the public record.

Search for "Michael Yeadon: His position on the pandemic and the loss of our civil liberties" if you want to watch the whole one-hour interview, it's riveting.

Here are a few select quotes from the good doctor since the beginning of the plannedemic, and there are tons more if you go looking:

"No variant differs from the original sequence by more that 0.3%. In other words, all variants are at least 99.7% identical to the Wuhan sequence. It's a fiction, and an evil one at that, that variants are likely to 'escape immunity.'"

"There is absolutely no need for vaccines to extinguish the pandemic. I've never heard such nonsense talked about vaccines. You do not vaccinate people who are not at risk from a disease. You also don't set about planning to vaccinate millions of fit and healthy people with a vaccine that hasn't been extensively tested on human subjects."

"I feel great fear, but I'm not deterred from giving expert testimony to Reiner Fuellmich for legal proceedings against authorities for crimes against humanity."

"By choosing this design (mRNA platform), the range of outcomes is probably 1,000 times worse than it would be for a conventional vaccine."

"Billions are already condemned to certain, unchangeable, and agonizing deaths. Each person who has received the injection will certainly die prematurely, and 3 years is a generous estimate for how long they can expect to remain alive."

"This is a conspiracy led by the central banking clique and their clients to take over the world. Once they've done that, destroyed the economy ... a great financial reset which will have us using our vax passes and digital ID, and central bank digital currency ... you won't like those, you really wont. It'll be the end of cash and any privacy for any transactions."

"Children are 50 times more likely to die from the covid vaccines than the virus."

With reference to this last quote, risk-benefit expert Dr. Toby Rogers did the calculations and stated *"So, to put it simply, the Biden administration plan would kill 5,248 children via Pfizer mRNA shots in order to save 45 children from dying of coronavirus. For every one child saved by the shot, another 117 would be killed by the shot".*

With reference to the second-to-last quote it's very clear that Dr. Yeadon is awake and fighting the installation of the New World Order!

He is also lending his expert advice and testimony to the current court proceedings initiated by concerned doctors, scientists and lawyers, with Reiner Fuellmich leading the charge. That's something for you to really keep track of, a real-life humanity vs. the NWO unfolding in court.

He is also lending his expertise in the scientific/doctoral world to America's Frontline Doctors, where you can get ivermectin prescribed after filing out some paperwork, ID check and payment. I myself did this and have two full prescriptions legally. I've also come across ivermectin(dot)com and you can access Ivermectin there even easier and cheaper.

Thank you, Doctor Yeadon. Your service to humanity is well-noted.

PETER MCCULLOUGH

I first heard about Dr. McCullough because as soon as he did an interview on Joe Rogan's podcast it was immediately banned by YouTube, about the same time as they banned the Dr. Robert Malone-Rogan interview. There was a bit of a dust-up in the Mainstream Media over this and Peter came onto my radar as someone I needed to know more about. What was his background and what was he saying?

When something is banned by one or more of the social media giants that means it is bad for the NWO agenda and should be sought out for us to decide if it is misinformation or if it is actually exposing the Illuminati's deadly agenda to cull the herd.

Dr. McCullough has been speaking out against the covid vaccine operation during the big vax-campaign-push and had attracted a lot of attention as his tone went from cautious at the start to full-on alarm bells to stop the vaccination madness.

Is he qualified to give his concerned opinion, or is he just a quack conspiracy theorist as the media painted him?

Let's see about his credentials here:

-Dr. Peter McCullough is a board-certified cardiologist and a Professor of Medicine at Texas A&M University

-He is the former vice-chief of Internal Medicine at Baylor University

-He is the co-editor of *"Reviews of Cardiovascular Medicine"* and associate Editor of the *"American Journal of Cardiology and Cardiorenal Medicine"*

-He has over 1,000 publications and 500 citations to his credit in the National Library of Medicine

-He is the author of 51 peer-reviewed publications to do with SARS-CoV2 infection (Covid 19)

I could go on and on but you get the point…he's vastly **_overqualified_** to be giving his opinion publicly about what happened. Not to mention he is motivated to speak up based on his ethics, not financial gain. He's an extremely well-mannered, well-spoken, good-natured, caring and compassionate doctor who takes the Hippocratic Oath seriously. He's one of the good guys.

So, what has he said exactly about the circumstances of the plannedemic?

Let's list some of his quotes and then we'll keep this report moving right along:

"We do know that COVID-recovered patients have a higher side effect rate when they do get needlessly vaccinated… Really, under no circumstances should a fully-recovered patient receive a COVID-19 vaccine … and authorities should accept that."

"What we had learned over time is that we could no longer communicate with government agencies. We actually couldn't even communicate with our propagandized colleagues in major medical centers, all of which appear to be under a spell, almost as if they are hypnotized right now."

"We have now a whistleblower inside the CMS, and we have two whistleblowers in the CDC. We think we have 50,000 dead Americans. Fifty thousand deaths. So, we actually have more deaths due to the vaccine per day than certainly the viral illness by far. It's basically propagandized bioterrorism by injection."

"In a sense, bioterrorism phase one was rolled out. It was really all about keeping the population in fear and in isolation and preparing them to accept the vaccine, which appears to be phase two of a bioterrorism operation."

"I published basically the only two papers that teach doctors how to treat COVID-19 at home to prevent hospitalisation and death. If treated early, it results in an 85 percent reduction in hospitalisations and death."

"Every single thing that was done in public health in response to the pandemic made it worse."

"Doctors, good doctors, are doing unthinkable things, like injecting biologically active messenger RNA that produces this pathological spike protein into pregnant women. I think when the doctors wake up from their trance, they're going to be shocked to think what they've done to people."

"Both the respiratory virus and the vaccine delivered to the human body contain the (cytotoxic) spike protein, the gain of function target of this bioterrorism research."

"If there were six things in the over-the-counter toolbox, I would put in there that Povidone Iodine. That's about $5 if you buy it online. And then after that it would be Zinc, 50 mg a day. Vitamin D, 5,000

IUs a day, increased to 20,000 a day during active treatment. Vitamin C, 3,000 mg a day, active treatment. And then Quercetin, 500 mg a day for prevention, 500 mg per day for active treatment. And then one last one, which is over-the-counter antacid/antihistamine which actually reduces viral replication and that's Famotidine or Pepcid, but at a high dose, 80 mg a day active treatment. So that over-the-counter list, if there was a shopping list if people were going to, in a sense, 'brace themselves' for Omicron, which it looks like it's going to hit everybody."

So, the last quote there from the doc was news to me that Famotidine was an effective treatment against viruses so guess who learned something new today…me.

Thank you, Dr. McCullough, yet another honest and ethical man making a stand for humanity.

CHAPTER 7

LOST IN TRANSLATION

"Pray, then, in this way:
'Our Father, who is in heaven,
Hallowed be Your Name.
Your kingdom come.
Your will be done,
On earth as it is in heaven.
Give us this day our daily bread.
And forgive us our debts, as we also have forgiven our debtors.
And do not lead us into temptation, but deliver us from evil.'

–Words of Jesus/The Lord's Prayer, Matthew 6:9-13

And also:

And He said to them, "When you pray, say:
Father, hallowed be Your Name.
Your kingdom come.
Give us each day our daily bread.
And forgive us our sins,

For we ourselves also forgive everyone who is indebted to us. And do not lead us into temptation.'"

-Words of Jesus/The Lord's Prayer, Luke 11:2-4

Why is Jesus calling the Name of our Father "hallowed," and what Name is it He is referring to as hallowed?

The word "hallowed" means greatly revered and honored. It's a very, very powerful adjective giving great importance to the noun being described.

It is used many times in the Old Testament, but only once in the New Testament, from the lips of Jesus, to describe the Name of our Father.

When you're done with this chapter, come back and read the "Lord's Prayer" again and you'll see it in a whole new light, halleluyah.

As with all information I encounter regarding getting at the truth of what is going on in our world, if I didn't think it was true and relevant to our situation, I wouldn't bother putting it into a book to bring to your attention to investigate further.

The information I've collected about this chapter for nearly ten years now would have easily amounted to a book all by itself, but these days we're short on time as things are moving quickly now. I only detailed and highlighted the subject but there is surely much more info than I am giving for you to discover and weigh on your own.

It seems to me that once again mankind has been duped of the ancient truth, driving yet another wedge between us and our Father/God/Creator.

Society and the world have slowly but surely abandoned His Ten Commandments via a slowly implemented deception, the Great Plan.

This is how the "Christian" holidays were slowly brought in by the Unholy Roman Empire after co-opting and merging Nimrod's

Babylonian Mystery Religion with the form of Christianity that existed at the time.

Literal Satanic symbols were also attached to both Judaism (hexagram of Saturn/Satan) and Christianity (The Tau/Cross of Nimrod/Tammuz/Antichrist).

And don't forget the rampant imagery of God/Jesus/Mary/etc.

"But an hour is coming, and <u>now is</u>, when the true worshipers will worship the Father in spirit and <u>truth</u>; for such people the Father seeks to be His worshipers. God is spirit, and those who worship Him must worship in spirit and <u>truth</u>."
-John 4:23-24

Let's just cut to the chase here: Organized Christianity, all branches, worldwide, are a complete and utter train wreck, completely under the spell of Nimrod, filled with his symbols and holidays. A complete and utter trampling of the first 4 Commandments.

You know? The first 4 of the 10 Commandments are directions for us how to worship our Father, not Satan and Nimrod, but that's how they've twisted it. Do you know what I'm talking about? If not, I'm going to show you now.

The following subject will be highly unnerving to some, and will probably elicit either intense interest...or recoilment back to the safe-space of what you were taught and shown all your life, which is all that you know.

And that's fine as this topic isn't for everyone, but we've come this far and we've got a little ways to go still.

You know me by now. I'm not here to sugarcoat anything, the truth is the truth is the truth, and if it's not, show me otherwise.

"And I will bring the third part through the fire, refine them as silver is refined, and test them as gold is tested. They will call on My <u>Name</u>, and I will answer them; I will say, 'They are My people,' And they will say, 'The Lord is my God.'"
–Zechariah 13:9

This controversial subject I'm going to take you through was brought to me by one of my first readers named Jonathan not long after releasing my first book in January of 2013.

He was very excited and truly in the Spirit about this subject that he himself had been turned on to by another, who had been turned on to by another and so forth.

Now. I'm open to anything I've not heard of, I'm after the facts and the truth because I want to live according to the truth and ESPECIALLY if it's backed up by Biblical verse.

I took in everything Jon had to offer and went to work like I do. I pulled no punches, dodged no facts, explored every avenue where someone could poke a hole in my story, and I always kept an open mind as you never know where you'll end up but wherever the most logical conclusion lies, that's where I'm going to hang my hat.

"Send out Your light and Your truth, they shall lead me; They shall bring me to Your Holy hill and to Your dwelling places."
–Psalm 43:3

"Teach me Your way, Lord; I will walk in Your truth; Unite my heart to fear Your Name."
–Psalm 86:11

God already knows how strongly I feel about this subject but I confess to you, friend, here and now, that I have felt GREAT GUILT over knowing about this subject and not putting it out there for you to at least be aware of if you wanted to look into it further. Literally eating at my gut for many years at this point.

In 2014 I originally intended to put this matter in a chapter in book 2, The Awakening, but that book took a dark direction as it was coming together and I literally ended up writing a book about Satan/Saturn/Azazel. I didn't feel the time was right and waited 8 years (!) until this book.

I could sense an over-the-shoulder pressure upon me when I committed to assembling and writing this book you're holding, and still do as I'm editing this, that this info needed to be put out there.

And if not by my hand, truly at my peril.

I will feel a TREMENDOUS weight lifted off me upon publication of this book, you have no idea.

Well....here we go...

THE NAME ABOVE ALL NAMES

I'm going to speak on the Great Plan-executed deception regarding the suppressed personal Name of our Father. The actual Name of our Father, the Creator God, the Most High God, was given to Moses during the same incident with the burning bush where Moses was called out to serve Him going forward.

Our Father's Personal Name is not some crazy tetragramma-whatever either. That's all smoke and mirrors from the occultists to muddy up the water and make knowing His actual Name seem puzzling and off-limits.

Those claiming our loving Father has a complicated Name that is disrespectful to use are ultimately exactly those seeking to keep you away from our Father for their own nefarious reasons...the proponents of the Great Plan.

Our God has a very simple, meaningful, powerful, loving Name that He gave us to use to communicate with Him...and then He commanded we use it...forever. Have you ever heard of this in your life? This is crazy that this is right in front of everyone's faces and hardly anyone is paying attention to this most important detail.

Our loving Father has a particular, personal Name...just as you and I do.

Just as my God-given (!) name is Jeffrey, He also has a personal "God-given" (!!!) Name!

"Your Name, Lord, is everlasting. The mention of You, Lord, is throughout all generations."
-Psalm 135:13

"Then I looked, and behold, the Lamb was standing on Mount Zion, and with Him 144,000 who had His Name and the Name of His Father written on their foreheads."
-Revelation 14:1

People call and refer to our Father "by name" as God, Lord, Yahweh, Adonai, Jehovah, Abba, etc.

These are the capitalized, proper-noun names given to our Father by man.

But what is the Name of our Father given by Him to man?

What is His Self-given personal Name? It's truly not "God" or "Lord" or anything else you've probably ever heard of.

Let's go right to the Bible verse where our Father reveals His unique Name to Moses immediately after first calling him into His service through the burning bush on Mt. Horeb.

Exodus 3:1-15:

"Now Moses was pasturing the flock of his father-in-law Jethro, the priest of Midian; and he led the flock to the west side of the wilderness and came to Horeb, the mountain of God. Then the angel of the Lord appeared to him in a blazing fire from the midst of a bush; and he looked, and behold, the bush was burning with fire, yet the bush was not being

consumed. So Moses said, "I must turn aside and see this marvelous sight, why the bush is not burning up!" When the Lord saw that he turned aside to look, God called to him from the midst of the bush and said, "Moses, Moses!" And he said, "Here I am." Then He said, "Do not come near here; remove your sandals from your feet, for the place on which you are standing is holy ground." And He said, "I am the God of your father—the God of Abraham, the God of Isaac, and the God of Jacob." Then Moses hid his face, for he was afraid to look at God.

And the Lord said, "I have certainly seen the oppression of My people who are in Egypt, and have heard their outcry because of their taskmasters, for I am aware of their sufferings. So I have come down to rescue them from the power of the Egyptians, and to bring them up from that land to a good and spacious land, to a land flowing with milk and honey, to the place of the Canaanite, the Hittite, the Amorite, the Perizzite, the Hivite, and the Jebusite. And now, behold, the cry of the sons of Israel has come to Me; furthermore, I have seen the oppression with which the Egyptians are oppressing them.

And now come, and I will send you to Pharaoh, so that you may bring My people, the sons of Israel, out of Egypt." But Moses said to God, "Who am I, that I should go to Pharaoh, and that I should bring the sons of Israel out of Egypt?" And He said, "Assuredly I will be with you, and this shall be the sign to you that it is I who have sent you: when you have brought the people out of Egypt, you shall worship God at this mountain."

Then Moses said to God, "Behold, I am going to the sons of Israel, and I will say to them, 'The God of your fathers has sent me to you.' Now they may say to me, 'What is His name?' What shall I say to them?" And God said to Moses, "I AM WHO I AM;" and He said, "This is what you shall say to the sons of Israel: 'I AM has sent me to you.'" God *furthermore said to Moses, "This is what you shall say to the sons of Israel: 'The Lord, the God of your fathers, the God of Abraham, the God of Isaac, and the God of Jacob, has sent me to you.' <u>This is My Name forever, and this is the name for all generations to use to call upon Me..."</u>*

The above Bible verses detail where and when Moses was called to be the greatest prophet in the Bible, to lead the Israelites out of bondage, and to be the inscriber of the Torah.

The fact that this encounter was also the exact moment our Father revealed His Name to Moses needs to be put into important context. This was truly an epic interaction between mankind and the Most High God.

Moses knew that in order to fully bring the Israelites back into the camp of our Father they needed something to rebuild the bridge that had been burned...something to reconnect them after 400+ years. Moses asked our Father for this, and the bridge was then (re) built by our Father via the revealing of His personal Name that the Israelis could use in worship, to call upon Him for guidance, and to render Him as much admiration and adoration as possible by following His direction to use His Name.

THIS IS MY NAME FOREVER, AND THIS IS THE NAME FOR ALL GENERATIONS TO USE TO CALL UPON ME..."

"Forever" includes today. "For ALL generations" includes everyone alive today, those reading my words right this second.

So why don't people call Him by His personal Name these days like He commanded millennia ago, let alone even know what His Name is?

Where in the Bible does it say we don't have to call Him by His personal Name anymore? Where does it say He revoked that command?

Where does it say in the Bible that substitutions for His personal Name are allowed?

Forever means forever, right? Right.

Use His personal Name to call upon Him, right? Right.

If His Name had not been important to Him, it seems He wouldn't have bothered not only giving it to Moses to pass on to the Israelis, but specific instructions regarding its existence!

In ancient Egypt, the incarnation of the Babylonian Mystery Religion at the time and full of 'gods' based upon exactly Nimrod and Satan, it was important to our Father to be identified by His Name in order for the Israelis to specifically call upon Him and no other god...which they had a bad habit in the past of doing! It seems a noticeable amount of the Bible is spent chastising the Israelis for exactly chasing after the riches and power of Nimrod's BMR!!

The Father did not want any gray area regarding the worship of the Israelis, not anymore at least. Either they were with Him or they were against Him via use or NON-use of the Father's name.

I'm going to tell you His Name now so I can myself refer to our Father by His personal Name going forward.

His Name, to the best of my research and understanding, is pronounced Ya-hoo-wah.

It is spelled in English as closely as possible as it sounds, Yahuwah, and alternately as Yahuah.

This is truly where the English letters "YHWH" come from (YaHuWaH), not "Yahweh" as has been told forever.

The name has been translated to English in the above Exodus quote as "I AM WHO I AM" which basically means "I am He Who is self-existent" and also interpreted as "I will be what I will to be". This is where the "I am" comes from when He is referred to in writing in the Bible, in discussions and lectures, in modern-day writings, and modern-day Christian music

The word itself, Yahuwah, is not only His Name, but the definition of who He is in our world. A very powerful, personal, proper-noun word that when voiced aloud, especially in groups reciting the Psalms, etc., gets His personal attention to collect up that glory in Person and I don't say that lightly as that is the reason for the Third Commandment.

When you vocalize His Name and make it existent in our physical world, you better believe He hears you so take this statement under advisement.

Nearly 7,000 times (!!!) our Father's actual, personal Name was REMOVED from the Bible to refer to Him, and substituted with the terms "God" and "Lord" and "Adonai" and on and on.

What happened over time is an abomination to Him, and He knew it was coming, and is EXACTLY the point of Him issuing the Third Commandment not long after making His Name known:

"You shall not take the Name of the Lord your God in vain, for the Lord will not leave him unpunished who takes His Name in vain."
-Exodus 20:7

Now replace our loving Father's personal Name in the above verse where it was removed and suddenly the Commandment takes on its real and fearful instruction. It was a BIG deal to our Father to mingle so personally with us that He would reveal His Name and He intended to protect it among His worshippers:

"You shall not take the Name of Yahuwah in vain, for Yahuwah will not leave him unpunished who takes His Name in vain."

Using something "in vain" means you're doing it but it is for nothing, the put-forth effort accounts for nothing to nobody. Not only a waste of time, but even worse an affront to our God.

The Third Commandment not only has a punishment attached to it for not following it, it also relates to the First and Second Commandments...

"Then Yahuwah spoke all these words, saying, I am Yahuwah your god, who brought you out of the land of Egypt, out of the house of slavery.

'You shall have no other gods before Me.'

'You shall not make for yourself an idol, or any likeness of what is in heaven above or on the earth beneath, or in the water under the earth. You shall not worship them nor serve them; for I, Yahuwah, am a <u>jealous God</u>, inflicting the punishment of the fathers on the children, on the third and the fourth generations of those who hate Me, but showing favor to thousands, <u>to those who love Me and keep My commandments.'</u>

'You shall not take the name of Yahuwah in vain, for Yahuwah will not leave him unpunished who takes His name in vain.'

–Exodus 20:1-7

As a side note in case you never knew, with regards to the Ten Commandments, the first 4 are instructions as to our personal relationship with our Father, Yahuwah, while the last 6 are instructions as to how to deal with each other as humans.

So what has happened since He issued these literal commandments that came "right from the top"?

With regards to the First Commandment, any number of "religions" with any number of gods attached to them have been in existence since before the giving of the Commandment and are in existence today, chiefly helmed over millennia by Azazel/El/Saturn/Satan and King

Nimrod/Baal/Zeus/Antichrist via the various incarnations of the Babylonian Mystery Religion.

And how about the Second Commandment? You walk into most churches today and what do you find? A picture of "Jesus" on the wall!! This is exactly the kind of deception Yahuwah warned us about. People walk right up to those paintings and pictures and literally worship that image!! A piece of paper they are worshipping instead of the Father and the Son!!

Not only that, but the picture you've all seen of the white, blue-eyed, long-haired Jesus is 100% NOT EVEN CLOSE to what Jesus would have looked like but another substitution...for a substitution!

The image of Jesus everyone is familiar with, arguably the most known image of anyone in the world save Santa Claus (King Nimrod), originated in the 1500s from paintings of the evil son of the diabolical Pope Alexander VI.

Jesus, a Shemite, would have factually had short, dark hair (Bible forbids long hair on men), brown eyes...and brown skin! No one knows what He really looked like, and this is the reason for no images as people literally worship this image of a false image!!!

This brings us to the Third Commandment regarding His personal Name. It is literally the only physical thing we have to represent, respect, honor and use to worship Him, and that too has been completely and utterly corrupted as you now know.

Putting His Name on a picture making an image and worshipping it is off limits, so the one physical thing He gave us that we were supposed to hold on to with respect to our Father was gradually but surely taken from us: His personal Name, voiced aloud:

"I am Yahuwah, that is My Name; I will not give My glory to another, Nor My praise to idols."
-Words of our Father, Isaiah 42:8

"How long? Is there anything in the hearts of the prophets who prophesy falsehood, these prophets of the deceitfulness of their own heart, who intend to make My people forget My Name by their dreams which they report to one another, just as their fathers forgot My Name because of Baal?"

-Words of our Father, Jeremiah 23:26-27

"I will vindicate the holiness of My Great Name which has been profaned among the nations, which you have profaned in their midst. Then the nations will know that I am Yahuwah," declares Yahuwah, "when I prove Myself holy among you in their sight."

-Words of our Father, Ezekiel 36:23

"And now this commandment is for you, O priests. If you do not listen, and if you do not take it to heart to give honor to My Name," says Yahuwah, "then I will send the curse upon you and I will curse your blessings; and indeed, I have cursed them already, because you are not taking it to heart.

Behold, I am going to rebuke your offspring, and I will spread refuse on your faces, the refuse of your feasts; and you will be taken away with it. Then you will know that I have sent this commandment to you, that My covenant may continue with Levi," says Yahuwah. "My covenant with him was one of life and peace, and I gave them to him as an object of reverence; so he revered Me and stood in awe of My Name. True instruction was in his mouth and unrighteousness was not found on his lips; he walked with Me in peace and uprightness, and he turned many back from iniquity."

-Words of our Father, Malachi 2:1-6

"Praise Yahuwah! Praise, O servants of Yahuwah, praise the Name of Yahuwah. Blessed be the Name of Yahuwah, from this time forth and forever. From the rising of the sun to its setting, the Name of Yahuwah is to be praised. Yahuwah is high above all nations; His glory is above the heavens."

–Psalm 113:1-4

"Daniel said, 'Let the Name of Yahuwah be blessed forever and ever, for wisdom and power belong to Him.' "

–Daniel 2:2

Because voicing His Name aloud in particular attracts His attention, the proponents of the Great Plan gradually replaced His personal Name with "God" and "Lord" and "Yahweh" and "Adonai" and whatever to cut us off from Him.

This had the effect of placing a dark cloud of deception over the world between us and Him. This has helped evil to prosper in the last few hundred years, allowing the Great Plan to advance by leaps and bounds. Look at where we are today, a completely backasswards, unholy world.

The less Holy Spirit that exists in the physical world about His worshippers, the easier the job of bringing about the return of King Nimrod would be, which is their ultimate goal. Otherwise, people filled with Holy Spirit would resist the evil, Satanically-controlled world tooth-and-nail. They needed it completely corrupted to accomplish their goal.

This is all part of our Father's Master Plan. That doesn't mean that our Father wasn't disappointed and arguably hurt to see His great Name disappear from His own book, the Bible.

What happened is truly a travesty and it significantly will contribute to His wrath at the End.

CHAPTER 7B

SOLOMON'S TEMPLE

Yahuwah's personal Name is HIGHLY important with regards to the rebuilt Solomon's Temple, the Antichrist, and the End, as the Temple was originally built to specifically "House the name of Yahuwah" (!!!)

Here is where our Father is giving direction for after He decides exactly where His Name is to be housed, representing where His Physical Presence on Earth would dwell:

"You shall sacrifice the Passover to Yahuwah from the flock and the herd, in the place where Yahuwah chooses to establish His Name."
–Deuteronomy 16:2

"...but at the place where Yahuwah chooses to establish His Name, you shall sacrifice the Passover in the evening at sunset, at the time that you came out of Egypt."
–Deuteronomy 16:6

"...and you shall rejoice before Yahuwah, you and your son and your daughter and your male and female servants and the Levite who is in your town, and the stranger and the orphan and the widow who are in your midst, in the place where Yahuwah chooses to establish His Name."
–Deuteronomy 16:11

"Then it shall be, when you enter the land which Yahuwah gives you as an inheritance, and you possess it and live in it, that you shall take some of the first of all the produce of the ground which you bring in from your land that Yahuwah gives you, and you shall put it in a basket and go to the place where Yahuwah chooses to establish His Name. You shall go to the priest who is in office at that time and say to him, 'I declare this day to Yahuwah that I have entered the land which Yahuwah swore to our fathers to give us.'

-Deuteronomy 26:1-3

"If you are not careful to observe all the words of this law which are written in this book, to fear this honored and awesome Name, Yahuwah."

-Deuteronomy 28:58

The most important standout to me regarding His Name besides Moses' interactions with our Father in person over the giving of His Holy Name, was what was said in the Bible about the Temple of Solomon being built to house His all-important-one-and-only-personal Name. These are verses in Kings telling of the importance of the Temple, the "house for His Name."

"Now Solomon formed a marriage alliance with Pharaoh king of Egypt, and took Pharaoh's daughter and brought her to the city of David until he had finished building his own house and the House Of Yahuwah, and the wall around Jerusalem. The people were still sacrificing on the high places, because there was no house built for the Name of Yahuwah until those days.

-1 Kings 3:1-2

The Temple was built in accordance with the first 3 Commandments. It was not built for any other god than Him. It was not built to house an image or likeness of our Father like the other pagan religions would do. It was specifically to house the only physical thing we are allowed to have to represent Him: His name spoken aloud.

"Now Hiram king of Tyre sent his servants to Solomon when he heard that they had anointed him king in place of his father, for Hiram had always been a friend of David. Then Solomon sent word to Hiram, saying, "You know that David my father was unable to build a house for the Name of Yahuwah his God because of the wars which surrounded him, until Yahuwah put them under the soles of his feet. But now Yahuwah my God has secured me rest on every side; there is neither adversary nor misfortune. So behold, I intend to build a house for the Name of Yahuwah my God, just as Yahuwah spoke to David my father, saying, 'Your son, whom I will put on your throne in your place, he will build the house for My Name.'

-1 Kings 5:1-5

"Then Solomon said,
'Yahuwah has said that He would dwell in the thick darkness. I have truly built You a lofty house, a place for Your dwelling forever.'
Then the king turned around and blessed all the assembly of Israel, while all the assembly of Israel was standing.
He said, 'Blessed be Yahuwah, the God of Israel, who spoke with His mouth to my father David, and fulfilled it with His hands, saying, 'Since the day that I brought My people Israel from Egypt, I did not choose a city out of all the tribes of Israel in which to build a house so that My Name would be there, but I chose David to be over My people

Israel.' Now it was in the heart of my father David to build a house for the Name of Yahuwah, the God of Israel. But Yahuwah said to my father David, 'Because it was in your heart to build a house for My Name, you did well that it was in your heart. Nevertheless, you shall not build the house, but your son who will be born to you, he will build the house for My Name.' Now Yahuwah has fulfilled His word which He spoke; for I have risen in place of my father David and I sit on the throne of Israel, just as Yahuwah promised, and I have built the house for the Name of Yahuwah, the God of Israel. And there I have set a place for the ark, in which is the covenant of Yahuwah, which He made with our fathers when He brought them out of the land of Egypt."

Then Solomon stood before the altar of Yahuwah in the presence of all the assembly of Israel, and he spread out his hands toward heaven. And he said, "Yahuwah, God of Israel, there is no God like You in heaven above or on earth beneath, keeping the covenant and showing faithfulness to Your servants who walk before You with all their heart, You who have kept with Your servant, my father David, that which You promised him; You have spoken with Your mouth and have fulfilled it with Your hand, as it is this day. Now then, Yahuwah, God of Israel, keep with Your servant David my father that which You have promised him, saying, 'You shall not be deprived of a man to sit on the throne of Israel, if only your sons are careful about their way, to walk before Me as you have walked.' Now then, God of Israel, let Your words, please, be confirmed, which You have spoken to Your servant, my father David.

"But will Yahuwah indeed dwell on the earth? Behold, heaven and the highest heaven cannot contain You, how much less this house which I have built! Nevertheless, turn Your attention to the prayer of Your servant and to his plea, Yahuwah, my God, to listen to the cry and to the prayer which Your servant prays before You today, so that Your eyes may be open

toward this house night and day, toward the place of which You have said, 'My Name shall be there,' to listen to the prayer which Your servant will pray toward this place. And listen to the plea of Your servant and of Your people Israel, when they pray toward this place; hear in heaven Your dwelling place; hear and forgive!

"If a person sins against his neighbor and is compelled to take an oath of innocence, and he comes and takes an oath before Your altar in this house, then hear in heaven and act and judge Your servants, condemning the wicked by bringing his way on his own head, and acquitting the righteous by giving him according to his righteousness.

"When Your people Israel are defeated before an enemy because they have sinned against You, if they turn to You again and confess Your Name and pray and implore Your favor in this house, then hear in heaven, and forgive the sin of Your people Israel, and bring them back to the land which You gave their fathers.

"When the heavens are shut up and there is no rain because they have sinned against You, and they pray toward this place and praise Your Name, and turn from their sin when You afflict them, then hear in heaven and forgive the sin of Your servants and Your people Israel; indeed, teach them the good way in which they are to walk. And provide rain on Your land, which You have given to Your people as an inheritance.

"If there is a famine in the land, if there is a plague, if there is blight or mildew, locust or grasshopper, if their enemy harasses them in the land of their cities, whatever plague, whatever sickness there is, whatever prayer or plea is offered by any person or by all Your people Israel, each knowing the affliction of his own heart, and spreading his hands toward this house; then hear in heaven, Your dwelling place, and forgive and act, and give to each in accordance with all his ways, whose heart You know— for You alone know the hearts of all mankind— so that they will fear You all the days that they live on the land which You have given to our fathers.

"Also regarding the foreigner who is not of Your people Israel, when he comes from a far country on account of Your Name (for they will hear of Your great Name and Your mighty hand, and of Your outstretched arm); when he comes and prays toward this house, hear in heaven Your dwelling place, and act in accordance with all for which the foreigner calls to You, in order that all the peoples of the earth may know Your Name, to fear You, as do Your people Israel, and that they may know that this house which I have built is called by Your Name.

"When Your people go out to battle against their enemy, by whatever way You send them, and they pray to Yahuwah toward the city which You have chosen and the house which I have built for Your Name, then hear in heaven their prayer and their pleading, and maintain their cause.

"When they sin against You (for there is no person who does not sin) and You are angry with them and turn them over to an enemy, so that they take them away captive to the land of the enemy, distant or near; if they take it to heart in the land where they have been taken captive, and repent and implore Your favor in the land of those who have taken them captive, saying, 'We have sinned and done wrong, we have acted wickedly'; if they return to You with all their heart and with all their soul in the land of their enemies who have taken them captive, and pray to You toward their land which You have given to their fathers, the city which You have chosen, and the house which I have built for Your Name; then hear their prayer and their pleading in heaven, Your dwelling place, and maintain their cause, and forgive Your people who have sinned against You and all their wrongdoings which they have committed against You, and make them objects of compassion before those who have taken them captive, so that they will have compassion on them (for they are Your people and Your inheritance which You have brought out of Egypt, from the midst of the iron furnace), so that Your eyes may be open to the pleading of

Your servant and to the pleading of Your people Israel, to listen to them whenever they call to You. For You have singled them out from all the peoples of the earth as Your inheritance, just as You spoke through Moses Your servant, when You brought our fathers out of Egypt, Yahuwah."
-1 Kings 8:12-53

The above quote is the public dedication by King Solomon of the completed Temple, built to house the Name of Yahuwah.

Not "God." Not "Yahweh." Not "Adonai." Not "Lord."

Yahuwah.

The Beast/Antichrist, a resurrected King Nimrod, is prophesized to sit in the rebuilt Temple of Solomon and declare himself to be "God". It is my opinion that he will take credit for all the various names of "God' as his own, except one if you know the truth.

"And the dragon stood on the sand of the seashore.

Then I saw a beast coming up out of the sea, having ten horns and seven heads, and on his horns were ten crowns, and on his heads were blasphemous names. And the beast that I saw was like a leopard, and his feet were like those of a bear, and his mouth like the mouth of a lion. And the dragon gave him his power and his throne, and great authority. I saw one of his heads as if it had been fatally wounded, and his fatal wound was healed. And the whole earth was amazed and followed after the beast; they worshiped the dragon because he gave his authority to the beast; and they worshiped the beast, saying, "Who is like the beast, and who is able to wage war with him?" A mouth was given to him speaking arrogant words and blasphemies, and authority to act for forty-two months was given to him. And he opened his mouth in blasphemies against God

187

(Yahuwah), to blaspheme His Name and His tabernacle, that is, those who dwell in heaven."
-Revelation 13:1-6

The reason for the blasphemous names on the head of the beast is because everything that people have been calling Yahuwah forever have been blasphemous names that originated from Nimrod.

The term "Lord" literally means the Canaanite god Baal, which originated as another name for King Nimrod, the original Sun god.

The term "Adonai" comes from the Canaanite "Adon", which is synonymous with Baal, which is synonymous with King Nimrod! Are you tracking, friend?

The Beast/Antichrist/King Nimrod will take claim for all the well-known names for "God" because they indeed are his names, just as he will take claim of all our "Holy" days/Holidays being dedications to him, because they are.

This will be the indisputable truth, and people will find no choice but to believe it and follow after him, not knowing the dark truth behind the truth...the intentionally hidden truth.

This is why it is at the top of King Nimrod's bucket list when he returns is to sit in the rebuilt Temple of Solomon/House of Yahuwah, claim that he is really "God", and blaspheme the actual, personal Name of the Father, Yahuwah.

The Father's Name will be blasphemed in His own House by the man substituted to His followers for His own Son.

"Antichrist" doesn't mean against Christ in the Bible, it means "in the stead of Christ"...an imposter. A substitution. A counterfeit.

The Abomination (something regarded with disgust or hatred) of Desolation (a state of complete emptiness or loneliness or destruction). This has to do with the profaning of the Father's real Name, that was long ago hidden and forgotten, causing great pain to our Father, inflicted upon Him by the followers of Nimrod/Antichrist...the Great Plan...the New World Order.

When the Antichrist steps into the Temple of Yahuwah and profanes His Name that Nimrod's people took away from Him, He will have had enough and Hell literally breaks loose on Earth.

CHAPTER 7C

HALLOWED BE THY NAME

"For I proclaim the Name of Yahuwah; Ascribe greatness to our God!"
–Deuteronomy 32:3

"Teach me Your way, Yahuwah; I will walk in Your truth; Unite my heart to fear Your Name. I will give thanks to You, Yahuwah my God, with all my heart, and will glorify Your Name forever."
–Psalm 86:11–12

"My Holy Name I will make known in the midst of My people Israel; and I will not let My Holy Name be profaned anymore. And the nations will know that I am Yahuwah, the Holy One in Israel."
–Ezekiel 39:7

I took the time to search the entire Old Testament for references from Him and His prophets of His Name's importance and there are over 200 references to the significance of His specific Name.

The book with the most refences to the importance of His Name was, not surprising as it's a book of praise and adoration of our Father, the Book of Psalms.

Psalms has over 100 references to the significance of His Holy Name, the most of any books of the Bible, and this is because it is showing us that to give maximum adoration, fear and compliance as He wants, you are to invoke His personal Name so that He hears you beyond any shadow of a doubt and knows that you are obeying His directions.

"If we had forgotten the Name of our God, or extended our hands to a strange god, would Yahuwah not find this out? For He knows the secrets of the heart."
-Psalms 44:20-21

"How long, Yahuwah, will the adversary revile, and the enemy spurn Your Name forever?"
-Psalms 74:10

"Remember this, Yahuwah, that the enemy has reviled, and a foolish people have spurned Your Name."
-Psalms 74:18

"But You, Yahuwah, remain forever, and Your Name remains to all generations."
-Psalms 102:12

"Your Name, Yahuwah, is everlasting, the mention of You, Yahuwah, is throughout all generations."
-Psalms 135:13

The Book of Isaiah came in second place with 32 references of significance of His Name. Is this why Isaiah is the most quoted prophet by Jesus?

"And on that day you will say, "Give thanks to Yahuwah, call on His Name. Make known His deeds among the peoples; Make them remember that His Name is exalted."
-Isaiah 12:4

"Now therefore, what do I have here," declares Yahuwah, "seeing that My people have been taken away without cause?" Again, Yahuwah declares, "Those who rule over them howl, and My Name is continually blasphemed all day long. Therefore My people shall know My Name; therefore in that day I am the one who is speaking, Yahuwah."
-Isaiah 52:5-6

"Who caused His glorious arm to go at the right hand of Moses, who divided the waters before them to make for Himself an everlasting Name..."
-Isaiah 63:12

You are not required at all to know the Hebrew language to talk to our Father by using His Holy Name. His Name is the same no matter what language, area, or generation you are in.

I'm sure you've heard the term "hallelujah," right?

The word hallelujah translated to English literally means "praise Yahuwah"... Hallelu Yah. It is LITERALLY praising Him by Name!!

"Yah" is the accepted, shortened version of Yahuwah, and I do believe this to be true and respectful.

I have a "Holy Name" version of the KJV Bible, which shows where His Name was substituted, but even the Holy Name Bible is not 100% on point. That's how deep the deception goes. But it shows where His Name used to be, taking out "Lord" and "God" and replacing with Yahweh. The "Yah" part is correct, but as far as I'm concerned the word is another red herring. I've found plenty of evidence for "Yahuwah" and little for "Yahweh".

Words and the particular sounding of words coming out of your mouth turning those two-dimensional letters into 3D, physical entities is HIGHLY important not only to the occultists when they are casting spells, summoning demons or communicating with Satan himself, but also to the Father and the Son and it has to do with interacting from our physical world to the supernatural dimensions of reality using these particular words we speak into being. Just as the beginning, when Yahuwah Himself "spoke" our world into existence using only His words.

Words and the sounds they make when uttered aloud are something that can't be passed through translating from one language into another. Those words were meant to sound like they were for a reason, because they had meaning.

Back in Biblical days, people's names had specific meaning, such as Isaiah (Salvation of Yahuwah) and Jeremiah (Yahuwah exalts) and Elijah (Yahuwah is my Elohim/God). The 'ah' at the end of their names specifically refers to our Father's personal Name, shortened as Yah.

Another example of this is Matthew the disciple from the New Testament.

The name Matthew was translated into English from the Hebrew "Mattityahu," which means "gift of Yahuwah". Matthew was specifically given to be a disciple of Yahushua (Jesus) and his name reflects exactly this.

And how about Jonathan, the man who brought this information to me to start with. Jonathan, originally came from the Hebrew name Yahnatan, which means "Yahuwah has given."

The Name of our Messiah was also corrupted. It went from Yahushua, which literally means "Yahuwah is salvation" to the Greek "Iesous" and from the Greek translation comes the English translation of "Jesus."

The meaning of His Name was literally lost in translation, but His original, Hebrew Name is precisely where the term "Jesus saves" comes from. It is the literal meaning of His original Name!!

I've tried talking to many people about the original, Holy Names of the Father and the Son and I'm largely met with blank looks and deferment.

People say "He knows what I mean," but these are the same "awake" people celebrating Nimrod's holidays of Christmas, Easter and Halloween.

I truly believe the people not using the Holy Names are surely saved if they believe in the Son's existence and mission, but that doesn't mean they are following His instructions either!

As believers we are tasked with keeping our wits about us as we operate in this Satanic world full of deception to separate us from the Father and the Son.

__"And He said to him, 'you shall love Yahuwah your God with all your heart, and with all your soul, and with all your mind.'"__
–Words of Yahushua, Matthew 22:37

__"Who has ascended into heaven and descended? Who has gathered the wind in His fists? Who has wrapped the waters in His garment? Who has established all the ends of the earth? What is His Name or His Son's Name? Surely you know!"__
–Words of King Solomon, Proverbs 30:4

Now, I would be derelict in my duty if I didn't reveal everything I came across in my research on this subject...

It says in Exodus 6:2-3

"Yahuwah spoke further to Moses and said to him, "I am Yahuwah; and I appeared to Abraham, Isaac, and Jacob as El Elyon, but by My Name, Yahuwah, I did not make Myself known to them."

I talked about the term that all those earlier generations knew the Father by in my second book in order to differentiate El Elyon (Elohim Most High) from El, another name for Azazel/Saturn/Satan.

There are a handful of instances, most notably Abraham and Isaac, where it says pre-Moses that Abraham had "called upon the Name of the Lord". The "Name" they knew our Father by was "El Elyon" and not Yahuwah. I'm just trying to head off an issue here and offer my explanation of the usage of the term "name" in those instances.

If names weren't important to our Father, then why did he change the name of Abram to Abraham, and of Jacob to Israel? That is fine for Yahuwah to do that, but by what authority does man do that to our Father's Name?

CHAPTER 7D

THE FATHER IN THE SON

Taken from the Holy Name of His Father, this is how and why the Son was named "Yahushua," and was called by Yahushua when He walked the Earth. Some people say it was "Yeshua," but that is the Aramaic version of the Hebrew "Yahushua."

At first, I had gone with "Yahshua" for a couple of years but changed to "Yahushua" after more research.

Yhe bottom line to Yah is that I'm making an effort to get closer to Him heading into the End. It is up to us to overcome any and all obstacles to reach Him.

The Name of the Son is not English-language "Jesus", which is a translation of a translation, and a name Yahushua never would have heard in His life.

The double-translated-to-Jesus name "Yahushua" has been stripped of its Holy honor and is literally void of all meaning.

Most people don't know that there was no 'J' in the English language until a few hundred years ago. No name of "Jesus" in existence before that. What is in the Bible was altered after the invention of the 'J', just as the Father's Name was removed.

Let's say 'Jesus' cryogenically froze Himself instead of ascending into Heaven and we woke Him up today. He would look at you with a furrowed brow if you called Him 'Jesus'. He would surely say 'I am Yahushua.'

Is He supposed to adapt to us? Our God??? Certainly not!

Do you think He minds that mankind took His Father's legacy out of His Name? And out of the Bible too?

When you meet Yahushua face to face someday, and you will, what will you call Him? Ieseus? Jesus? Or will you call Him by His Hebrew birth Name as He was called by Our Father and the apostles?

Some people say stuff like "God is powerful enough to keep the Bible from being altered." That is simply not the case after what you've just been shown! I would say removing His Holy Name is case enough for that!

If a name isn't important, why then has Yahuwah taken the trouble to create the Book of Life with your personal name in particular in it?

"Now at that time Michael, the great prince who stands guard over the sons of your people, will arise. And there will be a time of distress such as never occurred since there was a nation until that time; and at that time your people, everyone who is found written in the book, will be rescued."
–Daniel 12:1

"Nevertheless do not rejoice in this, that the spirits are subject to you, but rejoice that your names are recorded in heaven."
–Words of Yahushua, Luke 10:20

"Indeed, true companion, I ask you also to help these women who have shared my struggle in the cause of the gospel, together with Clement also and the rest of my fellow workers, whose names are in the book of life."
–Philippians 4:3

"He who overcomes will thus be clothed in white garments; and I will not erase his name from the book of life, and I will confess his name before My Father and before His angels."

–Revelation 3:5

"All who dwell on the earth will worship him, everyone whose name has not been written from the foundation of the world in the book of life of the Lamb who has been slain."

–Revelation 13:8

"The beast that you saw was, and is not, and is about to come up out of the abyss and go to destruction. And those who dwell on the earth, whose name has not been written in the book of life from the foundation of the world, will wonder when they see the beast, that he was and is not and will come."

–Revelation 17:8

"Yahushua said to him, "I am the way, and the truth, and the life; no one comes to the Father except through Me."

–John 14:6

"Yahushua spoke these things; and raising His eyes to heaven, He said, 'Father, the hour has come; glorify Your Son, so that the Son may glorify You, just as You gave Him authority over all mankind, so that to all whom You have given Him, He may give eternal life. And this is eternal life, that they may know You, the only true God, and Yahushua whom You have sent. I glorified You on the earth by accomplishing the work which You have given Me to do. And now You, Father, glorify Me together with Yourself, with the glory which I had with You before the world existed.

I have revealed Your name to the men whom You gave Me out of the world; they were Yours and You gave them to Me, and they have followed Your word. Now they have come to know that everything which You have given Me is from You; for the words which You gave Me I have given to them; and they received them and truly understood that I came forth from You, and they believed that You sent Me. I ask on their behalf; I do not ask on behalf of the world, but on the behalf of those whom You have given Me, because they are Yours; and all things that are Mine are Yours, and Yours are Mine; and I have been glorified in them. I am no longer going to be in the world; and yet they themselves are in the world, and I am coming to You. Holy Father, keep them in Your name, <u>the name which You have given Me</u>, so that they may be one just as We are. While I was with them, I was keeping them in Your name, <u>which You have given Me</u>; and I guarded them, and not one of them perished except the son of destruction, so that the Scripture would be fulfilled.'"

–John 17:1-12

So what does the New Testament say about the name of the Father?

Besides removing His Name we were supposed to use forever, not a lot compared to the OT. That's because the NT is all about the "new bridge", the Son, and how we're supposed to glorify the Father by glorifying the Son.

I'll leave you with this, from His Son:

"Our Father, who is in Heaven, hallowed by Thy Name."

CHAPTER 8

THE ENDGAME

"I don't have to tell you things are bad. Everybody knows things are bad. It's a depression. Everybody's out of work or scared of losing their job. The dollar buys a nickel's worth. Banks are going bust. Shopkeepers keep a gun under the counter. Punks are running wild in the street and there's nobody anywhere who seems to know what to do, and there's no end to it.

We know the air is unfit to breathe and our food is unfit to eat, and we sit watching our TVs while some local newscaster tells us that today we had fifteen homicides and sixty-three violent crimes, as if that's the way it's supposed to be!

We know things are bad — worse than bad. They're crazy. It's like everything everywhere is going crazy, so we don't go out anymore. We sit in the house, and slowly the world we are living in is getting smaller, and all we say is: 'Please, at least leave us alone in our living rooms. Let me have my toaster and my TV and my steel-belted radials and I won't say anything. Just leave us alone.'

Well, I'm not gonna leave you alone. I want you to get MAD!

I don't want you to protest. I don't want you to riot — I don't want you to write to your congressman, because I wouldn't know what to tell you to write. I don't know what to do about

the depression and the inflation and the Russians and the crime in the street. All I know is that first you've got to get MAD!

You've got to say: 'I'm a human being, god-dammit! My life has value!'

So, I want you to get up now. I want all of you to get up out of your chairs. I want you to get up right now and go to the window. Open it, and stick your head out, and yell: 'I'M AS MAD AS HELL, AND I'M NOT GONNA TAKE THIS ANYMORE!'

I want you to get up right now. Sit up. Go to your windows. Open them and stick your head out and yell – 'I'M AS MAD AS HELL AND I'M NOT GONNA TAKE THIS ANYMORE!'

Things have got to change. But first, you've gotta get MAD!...You've got to say, 'I'M AS MAD AS HELL, AND I'M NOT GONNA TAKE THIS ANYMORE!' Then we'll figure out what to do about the depression and the inflation and the oil crisis.

But first, get up out of your chairs, open the window, stick your head out, and yell, and say it: 'I'M AS MAD AS HELL, AND I'M NOT GONNA TAKE THIS ANYMORE!'

-From the movie "Network," 1976

The above speech perfectly sums up our world in both 1976 when the movie came out, and today as things have truly progressed for the worse.

It also reflects my position on the state of the world in 2023...I'm MAD AS HELL!!!

We are being robbed by the Illuminati and their underlings on all fronts and they made laws to make it all legal even though it isn't.

The prime example of this is the illegal-according-to-the-Constitution existence of the Federal Reserve.

Literally printing money out of thin air and loaning it at face value PLUS COMPOUNDING INTEREST to our Federal Government.

It is absolutely unbelievable and maddening that this is allowed to occur.

Henry Ford, founder of Ford motor company, said it best:

"It is well enough that people of the nation do not understand our banking and monetary system, for if they did, I believe there would be a revolution before tomorrow morning."

We are being financially raped daily. The Satanic Illuminati who literally own the Fed know which way interest rates are going because they control them and they use this advance knowledge to profit greatly in banking, real estate, and the stock market. They literally can't lose!!

They pirated from humanity all the money, which equates to power, they needed to fulfill their end of the prophecy of bringing Nimrod back to rule once again. General humanity has paid for the Great Plan from the start.

Now the Illuminati essentially own the Earth, control all the governments, and claim as possessions all its contents and inhabitants through the exercising of Marine Admiralty Law. Now THERE'S something for you to look into!!

Now that they own everything all that's left is to implode the fiat-money-pyramid-scheme and bankrupt humanity once and for all.

And I do believe we are at the end, both from a societal standpoint and a mathematical standpoint.

Everything is in place to initiate the End to complete the Great Plan...so they did.

CHAPTER 8A

END TIMETABLE

Soooo...I've got another controversial subject here for you to ponder...!

This isn't something someone tipped me off about, or research others had done in the past that I knew of, it was purely the result of my neurotic brain trying to figure out every aspect of the Great Plan... including the timing of the End as it relates to where we are today.

Many people of the past have predicted the End and the dates came and went and nothing happened. It's because there were still too many puzzle pieces missing, especially the technology needed to bring back Nimrod from the dead.

We have that power today, and recently no less.

In 2015 I released my second book, the Awakening, and in 2016 I edited out the information we're going to go over as I felt it was premature to talk about the subject of the timing of the End.

Given the state of today's world and everything I have learned since then, I feel the time is right to put it back out there in the public arena for discussion.

I incorporated my calculations using a fascinating book that I highly recommend you read called "The Book of Jashar," sometimes spelled Jasher.

For your reference, the "Book of Jashar" is referenced twice in the Bible as being legitimate, which is why I used it to try and verify what I believe we are staring down.

"...and he told them to teach the sons of Judah the mourning song of the bow; behold, it is written in the Book of Jashar."
–2 Samuel 1:18

"So the sun stood still, and the moon stopped, until the nation avenged themselves of their enemies. Is it not written in the Book of Jashar? And the sun stopped in the middle of the sky and did not hurry to go down for about a whole day."
–Joshua 10:13

The following is excerpted from the original version of **"Rise of the New World Order 2: The Awakening"**, released in mid-2015, pages 113–115.

.... The Book of Jashar is also highly interesting in that there is substantial information about King Nimrod, **including a scene directly between Abraham and Nimrod of literally Biblical proportions!**

King Nimrod, the founder of the Babylonian Mystery Religion and the Antichrist himself vs. God's chosen human representative whose descendent Jesus would be the very one to quash Nimrod's quest for immortality. I'll leave all those quotes for another book, or for you to discover, but there is one more item from the Book of Jashar that jumped out at me as I was going through it.

The Book of Jashar actually gives a timeline of the Biblical events, starting from the creation of mankind to the death of Joshua, denoting time in 'AM', which stands for 'Anno Mundi', which itself means 'Year of the World'.

By taking the date of the death of Moses, which is listed as 2,488 AM in the Book of Jashar, and comparing it to when Biblical historians say he died, we are able to work backward and forward from this date until we come up with a total of about 6,000 years.

It is my opinion that from the time mankind was placed here in the form we know him as today, to the culmination of the End Times, would be right about 6,000 years. This is because numerology is not only important to the occultists running the world, but because God was the one who made those numbers important to begin with.

It is my *opinion* that in this situation God is treating 1,000 years as a day in His world, and on the seventh day, which would be the seventh millennium of our existence, this will be the beginning of the Millennial Kingdom. This is exactly **why** it is called the Millennial Kingdom; it is virtually a **Sabbath Millennium** of global peace, love and worship of Jesus.

By taking the date the Book of Jashar says Moses died, 2,488, which is counting forward remember, and adding it to the approximate date theological historians say Moses would have died, which ranges from 1,450 to 1,270 B.C., you would get a range of 3,758 to 3,938 years from the time mankind appeared to 0 B.C. Add today's year of 2015 (2,015) and you would get a range of 5,773 to 5,953 of approximate years lapsed since the Millennial Kingdom clock was set into motion. **This would leave 47 to 227 (or so) more years to go until the Millennial Kingdom, which equates to the return of Jesus.**

The prophesized one world government would have to come immediately before this, **which is in existence today at the United**

Nations. We are only one global calamity from causing the nations to fully succumb to the United Nations as the true one world government of the End Times.

This global calamity will arguably be the global financial collapse that is coming. That's my front-runner in the big picture of things. It might not come this year or next, but it will come and it is being prepared for on many fronts, with the most visible being the ever-growing global police state.

While researching this theory that Jesus' return could be imminent, I came across the following verses to help corroborate my hypothesis:

"But do not ignore this one ****fact,**** beloved, that with Yahuwah one day is like a thousand years and a thousand years like one day."
-2 Peter 3:8

And also:

"Yahuwah, you have been our refuge through all generations. Before the mountains were born, the earth and the world brought forth, from eternity to eternity you are Yahuwah. You turn humanity back into dust, saying, "Return, you children of Adam!" A thousand years in your eyes are merely a day gone by...."
-Psalm 90:1-4

Sir Isaac Newton was also doing some calculations along these same lines on this, and he stated that the Millennial Kingdom would not begin any sooner than the year 2060. The dates above I'm giving range from the year 2062 to 2242.

I personally give much more credence to a date closer to 2060 as opposed to 2242, and when I saw his earliest date virtually match my closest start date, I had an epiphany we are truly near to His coming.

Newton obviously arrived at his conclusion the same way I did, but not finding this out nor the Biblical verses above until *after* I had considered the way I could make an approximation only makes this estimation all the more plausible.

<u>"It may end later, but I see no reason for its ending sooner. This I mention not to assert when the time of the end shall be, but to put a stop to the rash conjectures of fanciful men who are frequently predicting the time of the end, and by doing so bring the sacred prophesies into discredit as often as their predictions fail."</u>

—*Sir Isaac Newton (1643-1727) giving the date of 2060 as the earliest possible start of the Millennial Kingdom*

(end of Rise of the New World Order 2:The Awakening citations)

CHAPTER 8B

ANTICHRIST RISING

One thing quickly, when it seems like They are trying to impress upon us in the New Testament that the End is Nigh, is because it _was_ back in their day, and more so today.

When Yahushua was here, 2/3 of mankind's allotted time on Earth had already ticked by so They Themselves were living in the last 1/3 of the timetable...if you give credence to my End Timeline (lol).

So. I'm going to build on the End-timetable-scenario I just laid out, taking into consideration what I've learned since putting it out there in 2015.

Let's take the date of 2060, and work backwards according to the biblically-derived amount of time in a generation, 70 years.

We are using this number because of the importance of the timing of the End with regards to the parable of the budding fig tree in Matthew, Mark and Luke's books, and the relationship of the rebirth/replanting of the Nation of Israel/fig tree.

70 from 2060 is 1990. Israel was reformed by the hand of the Satan/Saturn-worshipping Illuminati in 1948, but **was not officially recognized by King Nimrod's Sun-worshipping, Babylonian-Mystery-Religion-following Vatican/Unholy Roman Empire until 1993.**

Don't you think that waiting 45 years is a little bit odd since Israel is so important in the Catholic religion and Christianity in general? That's because the Antichrist had them wait until the DNA technology was available to recognize it and set the Endtime clock in motion

Take into account that the Illuminati/Saturn worshippers have competed with the Babylonian Mystery Religion/Unholy Roman Empire/Sun worshippers for control of the Great Plan for Millenia. The hatchet was buried in 1993. They formally joined forces to see the Great Plan across the finish line.

Nimrod, the demonic king of the Abyss, is vastly over the heads of the human Illuminati in the supernatural pecking order. By Nimrod's authority, not the Illuminati, the generation of the End was initiated.

Nimrod sees all from his spiritual prison in the Abyss what is happening on Earth and directs his people to do his bidding through occult rituals. The all-seeing eye is the eye of Nimrod watching the Great Plan he initiated march along over millenia…watching and steering.

He could see his people had finally pioneered the DNA technology needed to bring him back from the grave to rule the world once again as prophesied exactly in Revelation. This technology was unavailable and unknown when it would come on line in 1948.

Only 3 years after setting the clock in motion in 1993, it is made public that scientists have successfully cloned their first animal using a sample of DNA, Dolly the Sheep….remember that?

Also keep in mind that black ops labs are 20 years or more ahead of what is put into the public arena. The Illuminati's DNA scientists and laboratories are literally the best that money can buy and far ahead of anything being performed at universities or the corporate world. While they announced publicly that a sheep had been cloned the black ops geneticists were perfecting their technique for cloning Nimrod from a sample of his mummified DNA.

So. Add a generation (70 years) to the 'confirmation' of Israel and the joining of the forces of the Great Plan, you get 2063, within 3 years of the 2060 date by Newton, and within 1 year of my date 2062, of the possible beginning of the Millennial Kingdom.

"Now learn the parable from the fig tree: when its branch has already become tender and puts forth its leaves, you know that summer is near; so, you too, when you see all these things, recognize that He is near, right at the door. Truly I say to you, this generation will not pass away until all these things take place. Heaven and earth will pass away, but My words will not pass away."

-Words of Yahushua, Matthew 24:32-35

This same scenario is also outlined in Mark 13:28-31, and Luke 21:29-33.

Yahushua is saying when the fig tree, which was established/planted in 1948, starts to bud and put forth its leaves representing life renewed, **THAT'S** when the clock is set in motion at approximately 70 years.

The budding leaves represent the means to bring Nimrod back from the dead…back to life! Literally renewed again.

It is my *opinion* that Nimrod was physically brought back into this world on 9/11/01, that was literally his re-birthday. There is much more to this than I have time or space to get into here about that, but I will expand fully at some point.

I do believe the Antichrist is alive today and is about 21 years old as of the publication of this book in 2023.

He wouldn't just be out wandering around though in public. He will be kept safe and secret until after the stage is set for his grand appearance on the world stage to save us from ourselves.

Oh yeah, there is something else attributed to Sir Isaac Newton I wanted to bring to your attention, a quote:

"About the times of the End, a body of men will be raised up who will turn their attention to the prophecies, and insist upon their literal interpretation, in the midst of much clamor and opposition."

And looking today at the state of the world without NWO-installed blinders…

"And just as it happened in the days of Noah, so will it also be in the days of the Son of Man."
-Luke 17:26

"For the coming of the Son of Man will be just like the days of Noah. For as in those days before the flood they were eating and drinking, marrying and giving in marriage, until the day that Noah entered the ark, and they did not understand until the flood came and took them all away; so will the coming of the Son of Man be."

-Matthew 24:37-39

Most people don't know the real reason for the Flood. It was not mankind's fault but the lustful fallen angels, including Satan himself, and their diabolical offspring, the 8'+ tall Nephilim. They were truly giant humanoids and vastly smarter than any man, so they took over the world after the fallen angel-invasion and made mankind subservient to them. Mankind just went along with what the Nephilim were putting out there for them in terms of direction…and still do to this day…from the king of the Nephilim himself, Nimrod!!

In both the Book of Enoch 1 and the Book of Jubilees, it tells us that the corrupted souls of the deceased Nephilim were shunned by Yahuwah and sentenced to be contained in the Earth as demons… that were allowed to interact with mankind once again…and were intentionally created to be used to test us, IMHO.

Nimrod is the most evil of them all:

"They have as king over them, the angel of the abyss; his name in Hebrew is Abaddon, and in the Greek he has the name Apollyon"

-Revelation 9:11

Apollyon =Apollo the Sun god.

Apollo was just another incarnation of Nimrod in the latest BMR empires, first the Greek, then the Roman.

There is a reason historians and the public education system globally call the Greek and Roman religions and others "mythologies" and it's to instill an air of make-believe about them, that they were just some crazy/fake religion that happened back in the day.

What they are successfully hiding is the blatant presence of Satan and Nimrod in both the Greek and the Roman mythologies versions of the Babylonian Mystery Religion. This is why they were giant, successful empires that eventually crashed and burned. This is all laid out very plainly in my second book.

According to Enoch 1, the final straw for Yahuwah to cause the Flood was the Nephilim were mingling humans DNA with animals, creating grotesque chimeras. They have been doing exactly this in the black ops labs for decades and now scientists are doing it publicly if you look. This is not good!!! We are back in the Days of Noah pushing Yahuwah's buttons!!

Unbelievable.

Yahuwah promised to never again flood the Earth but you better believe He's going to do everything BUT that to the world to vent His anger.

Since mankind now has the DNA technology to inflict the ultimate affront to Yahuwah, bringing King Nimrod back from the dead, you better believe the End clock is in motion!

"But realize this, that in the last days difficult times will come. For people will be lovers of self, lovers of money, boastful, arrogant, slanderers, disobedient to parents, ungrateful, unholy, unloving, irreconcilable, malicious gossips, without self-control, brutal, haters of good, treacherous, reckless, conceited, lovers of pleasure rather than lovers of God, holding to a form of godliness although they have denied its power; avoid such people as these."

-Timothy 3:1-5

The worst economic collapse in human history right around the corner in mid 2023?

Check.

Lovers of self? Ummm…okaaay…I think he means the ever-increasing pornography presence bringing lust and sin up to levels never seen before and beyond.

Lovers of money? Cha-ching!

Boastful? Of course.

Arrogant? Let's just get to the point here.

I think we can both agree, friend, that everything to do with the world Paul predicted would happen at the End is happening today and getting more indicative every day of dark times coming.

No wonder the young generations today are so messed up. It's not hard for many of them to see our future looks bleak at best and ominous at worst, and they don't know the real reason why. Intentionally. Or else they might wake up, band together and revolt against their corporate masters.

(hint)

CHAPTER 8C

DESTRUCTION JUNCTION

Humanity today is being coerced into pushing Yahuwah to conflict, angering Him more with every passing day...right up until the Abomination of Desolation of His personal, loving, righteous and forever Name.

What has happened in the last hundred years or so in particular with the advent of advanced technology allowing man to commit ever-greater sin will be happening with increasing frequency and scale in the near future.

This can't continue on His watch and it won't. For the second and last time, the curse of the fallen angels and their demonic offspring that went against Yahuwah will bring about the End for mankind.

It is because of Satan and his demonic horde that we needed Yahushua to pardon us for what was coming in the last 2,000 years of humanities' existence.

Part of the transgressions against Yah are being carried out today by meddling with the Earth's natural weather systems using Tesla's incredible technology via HAARP, soon to be used to cause cataclysmic events.

I've done a ton of research about Tesla's amazing discoveries incorporated into HAARP, the High-frequency Active Auroral Research Program.

This 3rd book was supposed to be telling you all about it but that will come hopefully with the next book as Operation Blue Beam is warming up in the bullpen.

I know what the HAARP tech is capable of and it's powerful and terrifying and yes, massively deadly if intended. Not to mention it is in the hands of the global Satanic cabal, but it is NOTHING compared to the power of Yahuwah. The elites truly did build hideouts under mountains to try and hide from what is coming.

I'll be honest and always am with you, I'm personally scared. Things don't look good at all for a quiet, peaceful future of comfort and prosperity.

It is all just reinforcement for my faith though, and I'd rather know the truth of what's going on so I can figure that in to my faith and life in general rather than be a teevee zombie, completely oblivious to our reality. And carrying on like that daily, just like Paul said it would be like at the End.

I'm fearful more of the Father's wrath every day as our time could be cut short in an instant with various catastrophic events coming, so make sure you are an asset and not a detriment to Yah.

These are some truly disturbing times. All this progressively-excessive evil is going on above ground out in the open and everyone generally knows about it, and can agree that it's happening, and even accepts...just like the scene from "Network" 1976.

They even joke about it in the mainstream media. Flashing all their Illuminati symbols and hand gestures to shove it in our awakened faces.

Either the people that are in teevee, movies, and music know what's going on and are in on the Satanism, pedophilia, blood/adrenochrome ingestion, sacrifices, etc., or they are woefully naïve.

The looks on the movie and teevee stars faces at the Oscars a few years ago when host Ricky Gervais mentioned Jeffrey Epstein and started making light of the pedophilia that lives in the shadows of Hollywood said it all. This is still on YouTube if you search for it. They all know it exists and accept it as the norm of their employment medium.

Whenever you try to talk to most people about disturbing stuff like this they immediately invoke the 'conspiracy theory' card to dismiss what you're saying because they don't want to entertain the fact that gruesome, despicable, evil acts are occurring and increasing in number and extremity.

There is plenty of evidence of this hidden evil if you go looking, and I have.

I'll never forget seeing a clip on YouTube, and it's still there at last check, of a woman on the Oprah Winfrey Show many years ago. She didn't use her real name and looked to be in disguise, and she said she was a recovering Satanist who had been raised in a real-life Synagogue of Saturn household. She had attended ritual murders and sex rituals and had been sexually abused herself as a child and into adulthood at these rituals that were attended by her own family and upstanding members of their community. Nobody suspected a thing.

She stated that a lot of the women (including herself) were intentionally overweight so they could hide the fact they were pregnant. They were having babies conceived at Satanic ceremonies with the exclusive intent of sacrificing those babies to Saturn/Satan, and were expecting to be rewarded financially for it. I'll never forget the exchange; Oprah asks her why they did it. Why did they kill those babies. She simply stated: 'For power.'

There are also numerous testimonials of former Satanists and/or people forced into it as children that escaped as adults. Their stories are both horrific and riveting, only reinforcing what we already knew. Some of these are on YouTube and if not there try bitchute or other alternative media but it's not for the faint of heart.

Unfortunately for us, these literal Satan worshippers run, steer and control the entire world through the power of money.

You will see and soon with your own two eyes what happens when the traitorous Illuminati-owned Central Banks overheat, collectively throw a rod and then disintegrate into shrapnel coming right at humanity…exactly as planned.

Pay close attention here, because when the dollar crashes and the fiat money system is done for, all commerce will come to an immediate STOP because people won't be able to do business. All food will disappear out of stores immediately and won't be seen again for weeks, months or more.

It will arguably be Martial Law time in that scenario. Not to mention the immediate introduction of the pre-planned digital currencies to try to get the world back up and running to semi-normalcy.

Things will be so chaotic that *"never-mind that the people who are offering the solution to the banking problem via digital money and accounts are the ones who caused the problem to start with"*… and also stole the entire planet's wealth and possessions in the process….FACT!!

But it won't be the Illuminati's fault though. Nooooo….that's conspiracy theory…that's crazy talk. Don't ever question the mainstream media/gooberment/central banks that are all owned and controlled by the …..yeah.

You will own nothing and be happy (to get a meal) is coming to be sure.

The fault for all of this will be propagandized and placed at the feet of the pandemic, the inept governmental response, and the subsequent botched mRNA vaccines…approved by the Federal Government's FDA.

"By creating many trillions of dollars out of thin air, the Fed set in motion an economic disaster. The warnings are over. Inflation is now here. Every excuse will be offered up as 'the reason' for economic pain. Don't be deceived. The unconstitutional Fed is the reason."
–Ron Paul

Besides the existence of the Fed, largely the reason we have such a giant National Debt was military spending to put the NWO global military infrastructure in place (bases and technology) and the globalist control structure in general. As you know, the USA is the global police and nanny state currently, but will be replaced by UN troops staffed by disposable third-world troops.

While the US was spending trillions of dollars in Afghanistan and Iraq for the War on Terror, China was spending their trillions building infrastructure to take over the world from the US. China will be the muscle behind the United Nations/One World Government, as China is their 'model' and people like Klaus Schwab aren't shy about telling you that!

"I think we should be very careful in imposing systems. But the Chinese model is certainly a very attractive model for quite a number of countries"

–Klaus Schwab

Allow me to translate from NWO-speak to layman's terms:

"We should be very careful about IMPOSING SYSTEMS…but… we are going to and it's going to be just like China's"

After the USA falls the UN will step right into our shoes and keep on going as the USA was doing before with humanitarian aid to countries, being the world's police, "peacemakers", etc.

The Federal Reserve private-banking-cabal is talking about going to a digital dollar. This will be the end of cash. Everything will be tracked. This will also make it easier to keep inflating our currency into the quadrillions eventually.

Ever see a trillion-dollar bill from Zimbabwe? I have and the number of zeroes in a trillion on a piece of currency is something else to behold. If they didn't eliminate cash, we'd have those in in the USA in a matter of time.

Keeping your money in the bank protected by the FDIC is a joke. Nothing more than a placebo pill to make people feel better about keeping their money in the bank to be used against us, which is exactly what they do.

The Fed is using the FDIC as a societal "calming pill" via the power of suggestion.

250 or 500 thousand dollars in cash, the FDIC coverage amount per depositor, is nothing in a hyperinflation scenario. FDIC has virtually nothing on hand right this second to pay back to the bank depositors in an emergency, the very situation we are told the FDIC will protect us from.

When you're standing in line inside the bank and see the golden-colored FDIC "Symbol of Confidence" logo to the side of the teller, it says at the left side a statement: "Backed by the full faith and credit of the United States Government."

Pardon me but "BWAAAHAAHAHAHAHA" ROTFLMAO!!

You just can't make this stuff up!! The "Symbol of Confidence"??????

No. When it goes you will see what a joke the Symbol of Confidence and what it states is.

Once the digital currency/social credit system is up and running after the dust settles it will be business as usual...or not.

The Chinese social credit system is the model the Illuminati have planned for the United States, and the more you look into it the more disturbing it is.

In China, all your data is on one app and the government can literally 'cancel' you with one click. Every action taken in China is under surveillance openly, unlike here where we have the same degree of surveillance but it is not out in the open yet as common knowledge.

You better believe everything you do is collected, snooped,filtered for keywords and stored in UTAH at the NSA.

If you haven't put tape over all the cameras on your phone by now, you're still living in the Matrix and you better believe those are recording 24/7 by multiple sources!!!!!!!

When you download virtually any app onto your phone part of the agreement is to allow them to turn on your cameras and microphones at will, not to mention see what websites you've been to, how often, and when.

Some, like Facebook and Amazon, record you 24/7 and all that info is fed into AI databases and mined to try and figure you out. What the layout of your house is. What products are laying around. Etc. etc. etc.

There was an incident a few years ago where a female NSA employee. Or was it CIA? Or was it Homeland Security? Hard to keep track of all the alphabet agencies, there are so many created to spy on us.

Anyways, this agent wrote a computer program to use the gooberment computers to intercept "dick pics" from across the communications channels that the feds can and do access at all times.

She ended up being caught with MILLIONS of intercepted images of male private parts so if you sent one to your significant other during her time of employment she probably had it!!

Let's see…what else is going on you should be aware of…

Klaus Schwab and the billionaire-boys at the WEF ran a cyber attack/grid down exercise in July 2021…so there's THAT to keep on your radar.

There will be some kind of major, planned event that will come along before it cannot be denied by society that the long-term side effects of the clotshots really are starting to show up en masse in order to have everyone majorly distracted to the point that the side-effects may be a moot point.

Think financial crash followed by the Great Reset!

If we get in a beef with Russia or China, this would excuse a false flag against ourselves courtesy of the Illuminati. They would probably EMP us, which would instantly send us technology-wise back to the 1800s.

What is an EMP? That stands for Electromagnetic Pulse.

When a nuclear bomb is exploded above the atmosphere, it releases gamma rays in all directions. The ones that head towards the atmosphere strike air molecules and strip off electrons.

Those electrons and gamma rays head towards Earth, stripping even more electrons. This avalanche of electrons, called the Compton Effect, interact with the Earth's electromagnetic field, creating very strong magnetic waves.

When a magnetic field crosses a conductor, electrical current is produced.

When this EMP magnetic wave crosses power lines, electronic equipment, anything conductive, current is produced. Enough current could be produced to create fires, exploding transformers, and extremely high voltage which can break down insulation and create arcing and short circuits.

In 1962 the US detonated a 1.4 megaton bomb over one of the test sites in the Pacific. It was high enough that the island of Hawaii, 900 miles away, had 300 street lights go out, and some microwave links were damaged.

Hours after the detonation there were still surges and ripples in the power system. That was when we used vacuum tubes and before transistorized equipment was on the market. Today, with microcircuits and all of the very high-tech equipment that we have in our homes, our factories and our defenses, we are more vulnerable than ever.

The U.S. Senate recently stripped funds for hardening the country's power grid against EMP from a homeland security bill.

We are on our own.

What can be harmed?

You, the human, will be safe. Magnetic waves, even very strong ones, will not harm you.

But anything with a wire or a chip. Whatever you see, be it toaster, TV, laptop, microwave oven, radio, chain saw, car, or truck, it is vulnerable, and the higher the technology the more vulnerable.

The cities' sewer plants would instantly shut down and immediately begin to spill into the streets. Could you imagine living on the ground floor of a high-rise apartment building as the sewer system utterly failed? Rampant disease would immediately follow. Riots, rape, robbery and murder would immediately commence upon those in the cities, especially if the guns are managed to be taken from the law-abiding before something like this comes to pass. The unarmed in the cities will be sitting ducks.

The EMP-scenario is a factual and most-likely scenario as nuclear weapons cause too much pollution/hazard for the Illuminati. Better to crash our grid and make us eliminate ourselves, and there have even been Congressional hearings and public warnings generated about this, so it's not a matter of if but when stuff like this is going to happen. The Feds even tell you to have two weeks of survival supplies on hand in case this exact situation occurs, you should have way more!

An EMP means that you won't be able to access your guns if you have a digital lock!!!

The circuits inside the lock will fuse together and become inoperable. Even if it in your basement it isn't safe. This is why I specifically bought one without a digital lock. If you do your combo and then leave it a certain amount from the last number the mechanical tumblers will not reset and you can actually get into your safe faster than with a digital lock.

If you do nothing else this year, have a locksmith swap out your electronic locks for physical on your gun safe...can't say I didn't warn you!!

The U.S. Government created a commission to study EMP and what it could do to the safety and security of the United States. Unfortunately, this Committee published its report the same day as the 911 Commission, so it didn't get much news coverage. You can read the report at www.empcommission.org. The bottom line in the report is that it is not a matter of 'if' but 'when' we will be hit.

CHAPTER 8D

FAREWELL FOR NOW

There is every chance that this is the last time you'll hear from me, but you should be all caught up for now, friend.

Please look for me on Facebook, J. Michael Thomas Hays. My other accounts were terminated on there and I lost control of my Samaritan Sentinel page and also "Rise of the New World Order: The Culling of Man's Meme Machine" page. They just drift aimlessly now but that's what happened to those pages!

I will eventually get on all social media under one or more of the names listed above, please search me out and friend me.

Thanks for your ongoing support, I sure appreciate you passing on that my works are in existence for those that have eyes to see and ears to hear. I'm not kidding about tweeting my books at Elon Musk either! Or Joe Rogan, I'd like to get on his show but unless he's barraged about me I'm too small of a fish. Same with Coast-to-Coast AM...they won't even return my emails!!

There is no shortage of things to look into and write about. Please pray that I'm able to pull this off, I want to get in there and fight tooth-and-nail for Yah and of course for my friends, family, country and YOU, my readers...the only ones listening to me!

"Who will stand up for Me against evildoers? Who will take his stand for Me against those who do wickedness?"

–Psalm 94:16

I really do need your help, too!! I'm purely operating via word of mouth.

I appreciate all my friends out there have done to throw in with me, leave book reviews on Amazon and elsewhere, and generally spread the word of my books. That is the single best, most-helpful thing you can do to give me a hand-up is to post book reviews for me on Amazon… thanks in advance!

On one of the reviews someone said they found my book through a TikTok video…good idea and thanks to whoever did that, I was unable to find it though.

If something crazy happens, I'll publish news and updates on my website, samaritansentinel(dot)com.

I'm not selling paperbacks myself but if I get das boot off Amazon for good and need to I will at that website. For now, it's a time-saver just having Amazon deal with it.

Special thanks to our new cover artist/friend for doing a great job, Andrijus Guscia with rockingbookcovers.com.

Also thanks to Eric "Spitfire" Wilkinson for backing me all these years. Our radio show was torpedoed by YouTube and every time we try to get another up and running it gets shut down. We'll probably move it over to Rumble or something but check my website and if we get something going where you can see and hear us in person I'll post links.

I hope to talk to you again soon, we'll see.

I don't know what's going to happen when I release this book but please pray for my family's safety...and mine!

Yah bless to you and yours and thanks for your support!

-Sentinel J. Michael Thomas Hays

Milton Keynes UK
Ingram Content Group UK Ltd.
UKHW010750110923
428455UK00014B/764